STRATEGIC PROPOSALS

Dunbar

STRATEGIC PROPOSALS

Closing the Big Deal

Robert F. Kantin

VANTAGE PRESS
New York

FIRST EDITION

Published by Vantage Press, Inc.
516 West 34th Street, New York, New York 10001

Manufactured in the United States of America
ISBN: 0-533-12657-6

Library of Congress Catalog Card No.: 97-91413

0 9 8 7 6 5 4 3 2

to Marylee
for her unwavering support
and encouragement

Contents

Foreword   ix
Preface   xi

  1. Selling and Strategic Proposals   1
  2. Client Analysis   8
  3. The Strategic Proposal   18
  4. Section I: Background Information   29
  5. Section II: Proposed Business Solution   44
  6. Section III: Implementation   61
  7. Section IV: Seller Profile   72
  8. Section V: Business Issues   81
  9. Important Proposal Components   89
10. The Strategic Letter Proposal   106
11. Format and Production   117
12. Writing the Proposal—a Partnering Process   130
13. Implementation   138

Epilogue   145
Bibliography   147
About the Author   149

Foreword

When I first met Bob Kantin, I was the newly appointed Director of Sales Performance for our organization. Bob was the "consultant" that someone within our organization had hired for a project. The project seemed very simple: design and implement a new proposal document for our entire organization. My first reaction was, *"Why on earth do we need a consultant for this? Just write the thing, and get on with business."*

As I began to investigate both the situation and Bob Kantin's background, I quickly realized two points. First of all, most selling organizations approach the proposal process in a very "backward" fashion. Secondly, Bob Kantin's approach not only made sense, but it had a dramatic impact on the sales revenue and profitability of every organization that used his process and structure. But there was an even more important and significant reason why I was intrigued: Bob Kantin's methodology behind his proposal process mirrored our very consultative, solutions-based selling process. We had just invested a large amount of money to research and map ours sales process. Yet, we were still approaching the proposal process in what I now view as a very "backwards" approach.

Our organization was not unlike many top organizations in today's marketplace. We were highly focused on our sales process and our continual efforts to refine and re-engineer it. But we were missing a vital component which would complete the process—*a comprehensive, consultative-based proposal document and a process to customize if for each and every sales opportunity.* The sales proposal and its effectiveness were always an afterthought.

In my book, *Increasing the Odds: Sales Is Not a Numbers Game,* I provide a gameplan for sales professionals who realize that it is not the number of sales calls that you make, but rather the quality of each call and contact, that will shape your career. Within this book, Bob Kantin provides the "companion proposal tool" for any sales professional who strives for the consultative approach when calling at high levels into client and prospect organizations.

As strategic selling continues to grow in importance in today's selling environment, understanding the significance of crafting an effective proposal becomes a considerably more important element in the process. Today's selling environment of partnerships's and long-term client relationships demands that you demonstrate a keen understanding of your prospect's organizations and their unique business challenges—along with how your proposed solution will help them achieve their goals and objectives.

This book completes the quality sales "roadmap" by incorporating the strategic proposal process. It will provide you with a competitive edge that you need now and in the years ahead. It also provides you with the tools needed to sell to a very high level within your client and prospect organizations—*a proposal tool and blueprint designed to answer the questions and concerns of senior management.*

If you want to dramatically improve the close ration of the proposals that you put into your prospect's and client's hands, read on.

—Bill Byron Concevitch

Preface

In the last twenty years I have worked for several companies, including two of my own. Regardless of my title, it always seemed as though I was trying to sell something to somebody—a new product or service, a new idea, or the need to start a new department.

I can think of several sales in my early career that were missed because I was not very consultative. In some instances, boilerplate proposals provided a panacea; there was no need to really understand my clients when I had an expedient means for packaging the price. Often I took for granted the need to fully educate my prospect on the benefits of the proposed solution—what seemed obvious to me wasn't as obvious from the buyer's side of the desk. Sometimes after a particularly successful presentation I would simply send a contract, believing that the client was ready to buy.

Ironically, some clients bought after receiving a poor or boilerplate proposal and others bought after my presentations and a follow-on contract. I know in some situations the sale was made because of the relationships that I had developed with my prospects or because I was selling something that really fit their needs. In other situations, I think the buyer did my sales work; someone in the buyer's organization did the analysis and wrote an internal report to buy; I simply was the one who took the order.

I was never lucky enough to work for an organization that taught its sales professionals how to be consultative and how to write effective proposals. Actually, none of the organizations I worked for ever considered the need to teach its sales professionals about effective proposals. Most offered basic selling skills and various levels of product or service application training. One actually recommended that a schedule of systematic calls, with no purpose or planning, would build a client relationship and eventually lead to a sale.

Over the years I read several excellent sales process books to improve my skills. However, it took a while for me to begin linking my consultative selling activities with the information in my proposals. As my integrated selling and proposal development approach evolved, I became more consultative and started closing more deals. Interestingly, I began spending more time actually working with my clients. My sales calls started lasting one to two days for some clients. My sales activities also became more substantive; I started behaving more like a consultant or business partner and less like a vendor. It became easier for me to write winning proposals because I was totally directed toward finding solutions to my clients' needs and objectives. Most important, my proposals now sold to top management because they provided the ultimate decision makers with all the critical information needed to make buying decisions.

As I wrote this book I had to reflect on some of my past selling situations. There is no question I would have been more successful if I had realized earlier that consultative selling and writing strategic proposals processes are totally synergistic. This book presents my approach for integrating them. It also includes very specific structure and content specifications for writing a strategic proposal, things that have worked for all types and sizes of businesses. Finally, this book introduces the concept that using a sales proposal model and supporting sales tools will make selling and proposal development activities much easier. These integrated processes, strategic proposal models, and sales tools work.

STRATEGIC PROPOSALS

1. Selling and Strategic Proposals

Proposals Defined

A sales proposal represents a written offer by a seller to provide a product or service to a buyer. All sizes and types of organizations use proposals in their normal course of business. For example, a house painter may give a homeowner a written proposal to paint the outside of his house. In this simple example, the proposal probably is more of a price quote than a sales proposal. But it may contain information that the homeowner can use to help select the right painter, such as the quality of paint that will be used, what preparation process will be followed, and when and how the painter wants to get paid.

On the other end of the spectrum, many companies write proposals for very large, complex sales. Their proposals often represent the culmination of consultative sales activities spanning several months that include multiple sales calls and extensive client analyses. Frequently, the proposed products or services represent strategic, high-dollar purchases for the buyer, the kind that require executive or buying committees to make the final decisions. This book presents an integrated sales and proposal development process for these proactive, strategic sales proposals.

Request for Proposal (RFP)

Some organizations must write proposals in a reactive rather than proactive mode; they receive a written *Request for Proposal* (RFP) from a buyer. The RFP may simply request a proposal for a product or service, in which case the seller can use one of its standard proposals and take a proactive sales approach in the response. Or, an RFP may clearly define structure, content, format, and due date; and restrict contact to specific people in the buyer's organization. In the latter situation, the seller must closely follow the RFP's directions or risk elimination from the buying process.

Responding to a detailed RFP is no fun. Ironically, the buyer's attempt to dictate precisely what to include in the proposal and how to write

1

it may actually thwart realization of the seller's abilities to present creative solutions and differentiate themselves. Although this book does not discuss how to respond to an RFP, it does include some sales proposal content ideas that may be helpful for a selling organization preparing an RFP response.

Consultative Selling

This book defines a consultative sales process as one in which sales professionals work closely with clients to identify opportunities that will improve their profits or reduce their costs. It is logical to use the adjective "consultative" rather than conceptual, strategic, or collaborative to describe a process in which sales professionals operate more like business consultants than vendors.

This author endorses any sales process or methodology that recommends sales professionals use a client-focused, consultative sales process to sell products or services to key accounts. This author also expects that a consultative sales process incorporates comprehensive analyses activities to identify and define the client's improvement opportunities—problems or favorable circumstance that the client has to make or save money. If sales organizations or sales professionals question the effectiveness of their sales process in these areas, they should evaluate converting to one of several consultative selling methodologies.

Key Accounts

This book will frequently refer to client accounts in complex sales as key accounts. One could substitute for this adjective "prime" or "major" to denote prospective clients in a consultative sales process. Further, the definition of a key account varies from seller to seller. For example, an independent consultant may view every client as a key account because each account is a critical revenue source. Other organizations might define their key accounts using one of the following definitions:

- **80/20 Rule.** 20% of the clients, the key accounts, provide 80% of the revenue.
- **Impact on Buyer's Business.** The seller's products or services

have a major impact on the buyer's business operations; e.g., a large, regional financial institution is a key account to a mainframe computer vendor or a manufacturing company is a key account to a consulting organization that is re-engineering one of their primary business functions.

- **Unique customer relationship.** Implementation of the seller's product or service results in a long-term strategic relationship between the buyer and the seller; e.g., a defense contractor that outsources their senior-level recruiting is a key account to a management recruiting firm that provides the service on an exclusive basis or the owner of a twenty-story office building in downtown Atlanta is a key account to a company that provides property and rental management services.

Process Integration

This author advances the idea that to consistently outperform the competition, selling organizations and sales professionals must integrate their consultative selling and strategic proposals development processes. Consultative selling means analyzing the client's situation and providing them with the information they need to make a buying decision—the same information required in a strategic sales proposal. Therefore, to be effective, sellers must integrate their consultative sales and proposal development activities. Their strategic proposals must actually document the results of their consultative sale process activities. More important, their proposals must position the sale for top management by including the critical business information needed to make informed buying decisions.

When sellers integrate their consultative sales and proposal development processes, interesting changes may result. In some instances reverse engineering takes place. Identifying the structure and content requirements of a strategic sales proposal early in the sales process may influence the sales professional's consultative selling activities. For example, if the proposal will include a sophisticated cost-benefit analysis model, then the sales professional understands that he or she must gather appropriate client cost analysis variables during the sales process. In this example the proposal's content requirements actually define specific consultative selling activities. The proposal does not dictate how to sell; rather, it helps identify what information is needed for an effective consultative selling process.

3

Two Important Proposal Functions

Whether the proposal presents a simple price quote or an offer to implement a complex product or service, it serves two important functions in the sales process. It represents a:

- customer communications document and
- decision-making tool for the buyer

Customer Communications Document

Some organizations may secure most of their business through proposals. Therefore, their proposals represent the most critical customer communications document they produce. For these sellers, proposals are more critical to securing business than brochures, press releases, or web sites that attract prospects but do not close complex, strategic sales. Complex sales require sales professionals to build consultative relationships with their clients and to analyze their clients' strategic needs and objectives. These types of sales require strategic proposals that communicate buyer-specific applications, benefits, and values.

Interestingly, some of the most prestigious organizations have little interest in the quality of sales proposals that are submitted to their customers. They often allow their sales professionals to turn out proposals that lack professional form and substance. One can only speculate why marketing departments, which are truly responsible for customer communications, do not support their sales departments in the proposal development process. Perhaps the reasons include internal politics or lack of awareness of the importance sales proposals play in communicating the company's message to prospective customers.

Buyer's Decision-Making Tool

The other key function of a proposal in the sales process is that of a decision-making tool for the buyer. Since a complex, strategic sale is information- based, the proposal must include all the pertinent information a buyer or buying committee needs to make a decision. This means a strategic proposal must be buyer-focused by defining:

- what is the improvement opportunity facing the client and how does it link to the buying organization's strategy,
- what buyer needs and objectives are associated with achieving the improvement opportunity,
- how the seller's proposed product or service will work in the buyer's unique business and operations—the buyer-specific product or service application,
- what benefits the buyer will receive by implementing the product or service application,
- how the seller will implement the product or service, and
- what makes the selling organization a good choice for the buyer.

Therefore, a well-written strategic proposal is a critical customer communications document and a decision-making tool for the buyer. It should answer more buyer questions than it raises and it should include all the information the buyer needs to know to make a buying decision.

Administrative Documents versus Strategic Proposals

Some selling organizations and sales professionals incorrectly view sales proposals as little more than administrative documents—just another obligatory sales process activity to complete at the end of the sales cycle. They view their proposals as nothing more than a document to communicate price and other seller information. Even though many of these professionals build solid client relationships during the sales cycle, their proposals are bland documents with little information to support strategic buying decisions.

When sales professionals think proposals are only administrative documents, it may reflect shortcomings in their selling skills. In other words, these sales professionals think proposals are unimportant primarily because they may not know how to write an effective one or how to integrate its development into their sales process. They may not know how to:

- gather the client information needed to write a strategic proposal or
- clearly define a client-specific application for the proposed product or service

Obviously, a sales professional is ineffective if he or she is unable to define what client information is needed first to qualify the sales situation and second to use that information to help the client make a buying decision. A sales professional also is ineffective if he or she is unable to define and document the client-specific application of their proposed product or service because it forces the client to guess at the application. Certainly, this behavior is assuredly not very representative of a consultative sales process. For example, a manufacturing company should not be expected to understand how an integrated accounting software package will work in their operation. The buyer would presume that the sales representative should have sufficient understanding about their operation to define the product or service application.

It is not surprising that those sales professionals who view proposals as nothing more than administrative documents usually write "boilerplate" proposals. Their proposals may be quite lengthy but contain little client-specific information. These sales professionals may think that they do not have to understand their clients to generate proposals. Rather, they simply make a few global changes to the fill-in-the-blank name fields and enter some other cursory information to their proposal template. No wonder that most boilerplate proposals read like poorly written brochures.

Ironically, if the proposed product or service warrants further consideration, boilerplate proposals often force buyers to perform internal analyses that define the application and establish its resulting benefits. These analyses often lead buyers to send *Requests For Proposals* (RFPs) to help them identify, select, and evaluate other options. Therefore, an ineffective proposal may move the seller from a proactive sales situation with little or no competition to a reactive, competitive sale requiring an RFP response. The ineffective proposal may put the sale at risk because it could generate buyer interest and raise awareness, but it lacks the critical information needed to make a strategic buying decision.

Conversely, a well-written proposal can strategically position the sale for the buyer, particularly for the buyer's decision makers, because it:

- defines an improvement opportunity that links to the client's business strategy
- defines the client-specific application of the proposed product or service

6

- presents client-specific financial and nonfinancial benefits that equate to real value
- presents a client-specific implementation strategy that minimizes the perceived risk associated with proposed change

Strategic Proposals Sell to Top Management

In many selling situations, the sales professional may have limited or no contact with the buyer's top management. Sellers are often insulated from the decision makers by their primary contact, usually a functional or project manager. Frequently, sales professionals do not even present their proposals. Typically their contacts distribute proposal copies to the decision makers and schedule an internal meeting to review all competitive proposals. Even though these sales professionals have good rapport and have built solid relationships with the contacts, their sales proposals represent the selling organizations to these decision makers. In all likelihood, the winning proposal will do a better job educating the readers, presenting compelling reasons to make a change, and differentiating the selling organizations.

Consultative selling and strategic proposal development processes are synergistic. Using a consultative selling process without an integrated strategic proposal development process will adversely impact results; an organization's proposal close ratios may never exceed 25 to 30 percent. Sales professionals may do everything right during the sale, but if they don't integrate the development of a strong, strategic proposal into the process, they put their sales at risk.

Conversely, sales professionals who use a strategic proposal model without following good consultative selling practices also may adversely impact results. They will skip sales process steps and move quickly to writing a proposal, their sales process crutch. Their proposals will include reasons to make a change, but they will lack depth. These sales professionals may even overlook the need to thoroughly qualify their prospects. Consultative selling and strategic proposals development represent synergistic processes that when correctly used will produce spectacular results.

7

2. Client Analysis

Gathering and Analyzing Client Information

In-depth client knowledge provides the foundation for consultative selling and developing strategic sales proposals. A sales professional never has sufficient client knowledge from the start. But, by using good consultative selling skills, he or she will gather appropriate information throughout the sales process. Further, the client information and analyses requirements of the seller's strategic proposal will help focus information gathering activities. In some sales situations, these proposal information requirements may actually control what is gathered. Keep in mind, if a strategic proposal documents the results of a consultative sales process, then the proposal's content will strongly influence what client information to gather.

Five Categories of Client Information to Gather

The many consultative sales process books provide a plethora of ideas for gathering client information. These books contain helpful tips for asking questions, ideas for becoming a good listener, and suggested topics for gathering information. A sales professional might begin to formulate client information requirements in five categories if he or she is selling a complex product or service:

1. basic client information
2. relevant strategies and tactics
3. product or service application information
4. financial impact measures
5. decision-making process information

Basic Client Information

A salesperson can gather much of the basic client information he or she needs before making the first sales call. This information category includes:

- client name and address
- primary and secondary contact names, titles, mail and E-mail addresses, and phone and fax numbers
- business/industry: type, size, trends, and competition
- annual revenues, net profits, number of locations, and number of employees

There are numerous, readily-available sources for obtaining basic client information: annual reports, professional and trade journals, magazine articles, internal marketing reports, trade-show lead cards, the Internet, etc.

Relevant Strategies and Tactics

The operative word in this information category is *relevant*. A sales professional needs to identify and understand client strategy and the supporting tactics that have relevancy to the product or service being proposed. For example, a large healthcare provider's national acquisition strategy is very relevant to a company selling software integration products. However, this national acquisition strategy probably has little relevance to a smaller organization providing audits of a local electric utility company. Perhaps the guideline to follow is that a sales professional should not be uninterested in discovering irrelevant client strategies; rather, he or she should be most interested in identifying relevant strategies. The definition of a relevant client strategy is any strategy that ultimately supports the purchase of the product or service being sold.

Supporting tactics are used to implement strategies and ultimately determine client needs and objectives. For example, developing profiles of corporate acquisition candidates is one tactic the healthcare provider might use to implement its national acquisition strategy. Implementing this supporting tactic might result in the need for the healthcare provider to build a corporate acquisition candidate database and ranking system. The organization also might establish an objective to have this database and ranking system operational in three months. Therefore, understanding the client's relevant strategies and tactics gives the consultative sales professional a critical advantage. It provides insight into clearly identifying those client needs and objectives that can be satisfied by implementing their company's product or service.

Product or Service Application Information

Some sales professionals think gathering client information to define the application of the proposed product or service is easy. In reality, this information category may present the greatest challenge for many sellers. It requires two important selling capabilities:

- in-depth product or service knowledge and
- the ability to envision how the proposed product could be installed or the proposed service could be implemented for the client—the client-specific application.

In some respects, the process for gathering information in this category compares to a civil engineer designing a bridge. A good engineer can visualize how the bridge will look when completed but has to do extensive site analysis and surveying before producing the blueprint to build it. A sales professional follows the same process; he or she can visualize how the product or service will be implemented but needs to analyze the client's business to clearly define a client-specific application. Knowing what to look for in a client's business and what questions to ask represent critical consultative selling and strategic proposal development skills.

To learn how to gather and analyze product or service application information, a sales professional will need to:

- study and work hard at gaining product or service knowledge,
- spend time with existing clients to learn about their unique applications of the product or service,
- listen to internal and external product or service experts, and
- ask lots of questions

The key to success is knowing what variables in the client's business define the product or service application and how they define it. For example, a sales professional for a PC training company that offers courses for standard desktop software such as word-processing and spreadsheet sys-

10

tems would probably need to gather the following client-specific information to propose a unique training program—the service application:

- software titles and their releases
- frequency for installing new releases
- number of users for each software title
- estimated user proficiency (number of beginner, intermediate, and advanced users)
- user locations
- available training facilities by location

By gathering this information, the sales professional will be able to define the unique application of their training services. The resulting client-focused proposal would include:

- which courses and what course levels will be offered,
- how many users (employees) will take each course and level,
- when and where the courses will be given, and
- what facilities and equipment will be needed to deliver the courses.

Obviously, an effective sales professional for this PC training services company must possess the skills required to define client-specific training applications.

Selling more complex products or services requires sales professionals to spend large amounts of time gathering and analyzing the information needed to define a unique product or service application. For example, a company that develops training courses for proprietary software applications would need to gather the following client information before proposing a custom courseware project:

- software application
- key software functions
- number and types of end-users
- training needs by end-user type
- pre- and post-testing requirements by end-user type
- estimated training duration by function, topic, and course
- delivery requirements: instructor-led, computer-based, or multimedia

Obviously, selling courseware development services for a client's proprietary system is more involved than selling training for standard PC software applications. The sales professionals for the proprietary training development services will require more advanced selling skills than those needed to sell standard desktop software. This doesn't mean someone selling PC training can't sell proprietary training development services; it means he or she needs to acquire more advanced sales skills.

Financial Impact Measures

To understand the true magnitude of the client's improvement opportunity, a sales professional needs to analyze its financial impact on the client's business. In other words, what added costs or missed revenues can be attributed to the opportunity. This can be a difficult exercise in some selling situations because the client may not have the means or desire to measure the financial impact. In other situations, the client may not want to release the information needed. However, when a strategic proposal includes the added costs or missed revenues associated with the improvement opportunity, it provides an ideal basis for calculating the financial benefits of the proposed product or service.

To understand how to measure the financial impact of the client's improvement opportunity, the sales professional first needs to understand how the application of the proposed product or service can make or save money. Next he or she must develop a financial benefits calculation and identify which client financial measures or variables are used in the calculation. After the variables are identified, the sales professional needs to gather this financial information as part of the consultative sales process.

For example, a sales professional for a paging company knows that its alphanumeric paging service offers its users the ability to send meaningful text messages to individuals. One of its prospects is a regional trucking company that is losing freight revenues because it cannot contact its drivers once they are en route. As a result, they are missing opportunities to reroute partially loaded trucks to pick up freight after they have left the company terminals or intermediate client locations. To understand how much alphanumeric paging services can benefit this trucking company, a sales professional first needs to define the financial benefits calculation and its variables for this client. The calculation would certainly include some of the following client-specific variables:

- revenue per mile
- average current capacity utilization per truck
- estimated revenue miles lost per truck per month because of inadequate driver communications

A resulting strategic proposal would use the above variables to calculate:

- estimated lost revenue,
- estimated revenue that will be gained because of the alphanumeric pagers, and
- return on investment comparing the cost of alphanumeric pagers to the estimated additional freight revenues generated because of better driver communications.

Having the ability to define financial impact of the improvement opportunity reinforces the need for sales professionals to have solid application and product or service knowledge. It's impossible to define client-specific financial benefits without first understanding how the product or service will work in the client's business. Therefore, an effective sales professional must constantly evaluate his or her product's application potential for each client, a critical consultative selling skill and certainly a skill needed to develop winning sales proposals.

Decision-Making Process Information

Although a sales professional cannot change the buyer's decision-making process, he or she can adjust his or her sales process and the content of the strategic proposal to gain a competitive advantage. To do so, a sales professional must understand the client's decision-making process in two key areas:

- who will make the buying decision and how might each decision maker influence the decision and
- what are the buyer's criteria for selecting a vendor.

It's important for a sales professional to know who will make the buying decision and how each member will influence the decision. For most complex sales, a designated buying committee rather than one individual makes the final buying decision. A sales professional rarely has an opportunity to meet with every committee member and certainly cannot expect to build rapport or develop a relationship with each. However, a sales professional's primary client contact will know how the buying process works and who is on the buying committee. Careful questioning of the contact will often provide some insight into how each member might influence the decision.

For example, if the company's Chief Financial Officer is on the buying committee, she might be favorably influenced by supporting financial analyses. If another committee member has a strong operations background, he might be influenced by a solid implementation methodology for the proposed product or service. The goal for identifying the buying committee is to tailor the sale and the strategic proposal to favorably influence as many of their decisions as possible.

Selection Criteria

Most buyers use selection criteria to evaluate and compare vendors. These criteria give buyers a means to differentiate vendors from their products and services. In some instances, clients will have a matrix of well-defined selection criteria. However, it is more typical for buyers to use an undefined list of selection criteria. Some common criteria include:

- seller's reputation in the industry or profession
- clients of similar size and/or type
- availability of verifiable client references

The more complex the sale and probably the more client-specific the application, the more likely it will be to find clients with very unique selection criteria. For example, a company evaluating accounting services may only want to work with a *second-tier* accounting firm that has international experience; two very specific selection criteria that quickly narrow the field. Another example of a unique selection criteria might be for a company evaluating PC training providers. Since this company has offices in twenty cities across the country and wants all employees to get the same quality of instructor-led training, it may only consider PC training providers who have branch or franchise offices in the same twenty cities.

Selection criteria provide good insight into part of a client's decision-making process. Knowing the individual criteria reveals what is truly important to the client. By identifying and rank- ordering selection criteria, a sales professional can:

- focus his or her sales activities to address the most important selection issues and
- tailor the strategic proposal to emphasize those seller profile components for which the selling organization clearly has a competitive advantage

For example, the top three selection criteria for a healthcare provider evaluating integration software vendors are:

- customer service and support
- continuing software enhancements
- product quality

A sales professional could certainly address these criteria during the sales process. Perhaps a trip to the software vendor's corporate offices to meet key customer service personnel and R&D staff might satisfy many client issues. However, the sales proposal provides an opportunity to clearly document a vendor's competitive advantage in those areas most important to the client. For example, the proposal should include the following subsections to address selection criteria:

- the seller's mission statement if it emphasized the company's enthusiasm for serving its customers
- a chronological synopsis of software enhancements and increased functionality from first software release date
- an overview of the company's quality initiatives, programs, and awards

After identifying and rank-ordering a client's selection criteria, some sellers analyze their relative competitive advantages, or disadvantages, using the top criterion as a basis. By knowing what importance the buyer

15

Selection Criteria	Rank	Client's Logic or Reasoning
Other clients of similar size		
Seller's Reputation		
Pricing		
Client references		
Software functionality		
Availability of professionals services		
Quality		
Training		
Customer service		
Annual Maintenance / Upgrades / Releases		

places on various vendor selection criteria, the selling organization can highlight those areas that the customer thinks are most important and in which it clearly has a competitive advantage.

Sales Tools

Thorough client analysis represents a major challenge for the best sales professionals. It is a key component of any consultative sales process and provides the essential information for writing a winning, strategic proposal. To ensure that their sales professionals are prepared to handle this challenge, some selling organizations develop:

- model proposals for their products and services and

16

- client questionnaires and product or service application work-sheets

The model proposals define buyer information requirements for the sales process. The questionnaire and application worksheets guide the analyses activities and provide a vehicle for inputting buyer-specific information to the sales proposal models.

Chapter 13 *Implementation* will discuss how these sales tools support the successful integration of a company's consultative sales and strategic proposal development processes.

3. The Strategic Proposal

Purpose

A strategic proposal sells to top management by educating its readers, the decision makers, about the improvement opportunity, the business solution available for achieving the opportunity, and other critical information needed to make the buying decision. The one-size-fits-all or "boilerplate" proposal does not work for a strategic sale to a key account; just like slick brochures, canned presentations, and trial close questions do not close complex sales. Rather, complex sales and key accounts require buyer-specific solutions, not generic product or service descriptions and sales-driven hype.

A strategic proposal is designed to:

- document the consultative sales analyses activities
- demonstrate a perfect match between the buyer's strategic needs and objectives and the unique application of the seller's products and/or services in the buyer's business
- provide indisputable financial justification for selling at desirable margins
- assure the buyer that the seller has the know-how, capabilities, and capacities to deliver
- become the basis for continuing improvement opportunities with the key account

Consultative Sales Process and Partnership Deliverable

A deliverable represents an end product whether it is the result of one project phase or an entire project. In a consultative sales process the buyer and seller comprise an informal partnership. Their partnering activities focus on identifying improvement opportunities that the buyer can achieve through the application of the seller's products or services. During the sales process the partners analyze and document a profit enhancement, cost reduction, or productivity improvement opportunity in a strategic proposal. This proposal defines the improvement opportunity and the proposed solution and links both to the buyer's strategy. It represents a sales process deliverable because it documents the partnership's activities. When the partners present the strategic proposal to the buyer's decision makers they are requesting approval to proceed to the next sales process phase—implementation.

The strategic proposal epitomizes consultative selling because it:

- defines the buyer's favorable or unfavorable circumstances and their linkage to the buyer's strategy—the basis for an improvement opportunity project
- presents a client-specific application of the seller's proposed product or service and defines the qualitative and quantitative value the buyer will realize
- describes how the buyer and seller will work together to implement the proposed solution
- profiles the seller's business practices—their ability to perform on the contract
- presents specific business issues associated with the sale

A strategic proposal provides compelling reasons for making a change. Without it, sales professionals often find it difficult to move many key accounts beyond prospect status. A well-written proposal will strategically position the sale for top management because it provides all the information they need to make an educated buying decision.

Providing Critical Financial Justification

A strategic proposal effectively communicates increased profits, reduced costs, or improved productivity to the buyer's decision makers. It presents the financial logic and analyses needed to support a buying decision. A strategic proposal makes the decision much easier because it clearly presents buyer-specific financial benefits provided by the proposed product or service. It does not make generic financial benefits statements, e.g., installing the widget will reduce production costs, adding the service will increase revenues, and training employees will improve productivity.

19

Rather, a strategic proposal specifically defines how much value the seller's product or service will add to the buyer's operation.

To better understand the concept of the proposal as a deliverable, it might be helpful to examine what happens when buyers and sellers do not form sales partnerships and sales professionals do not follow a consultative sales process; sellers either (1) do not write proposals or (2) write boilerplate proposals.

No Proposal

It is very difficult for buyers to make informed buying decisions when sellers fail to write proposals. When the decision makers do not have sufficient information, they may decide not to buy or they may decide to delay the buying decision. They simply are not comfortable making a decision when they lack sufficient information.

Conversely, a well-crafted, strategic proposal helps management make informed buying decisions because it provides all the background, logic, and justification for moving forward. The proposal clearly defines the improvement opportunity, the seller's proposed solution, and financial and nonfinancial benefits for moving forward.

In a situation in which the seller does not provide a proposal but the buyer thinks the seller's solution has merit, one of the buyer's managers may write an internal sales proposal, also known as a "recommendation report." Certainly a seller jeopardizes the sale when he forces the buyer to develop some type of internal proposal. The seller loses control of the sales message and the improvement opportunity analyses. Compared to a well-written sales proposal, most internal recommendation reports lack the sophisticated application dimensions that only an experienced, consultative sales professional can develop. Further, because most buyers will lack in-depth product or service knowledge, they may be unable to develop the compelling financial justifications needed to support a buying decision.

For example, the largest data processing firms would have few outsourcing customers if they did not write strategic proposals. To get a contract without a proposal would mean their prospective customers would have to either blindly accept a price quotation or complete an internal recommendation report based upon the price. Given the size, complexity, and strategic implications of most outsourcing contracts, both alternatives are highly unlikely.

Boilerplate Proposal

Boilerplate proposals are ineffective for key accounts sales because they send several undesirable messages:

- All buyers are the same: the seller does not consider the buyer a key account—the buyer does not warrant the commitment of the seller's time to understand their unique business strategies and operations
- The seller has inexperienced, unknowledgeable sales professionals: the sales professional lacks the knowledge and experience needed to understand the buyer's strategies, identify an improvement opportunity, and define a custom application of the proposed product or service.
- Commodity selling: the seller cannot differentiate their product or service other than by price; commodity selling

When a selling organization uses a boilerplate proposal, their intent is usually to:

- deliver consistent, generic sales messages that ensure their sales professionals correctly communicate generic product features or service capabilities
- ensure that each proposal contains standardized wording to comply with some legal or disclosure requirements
- avoid providing sales professionals with the systems, training, and support required to develop winning proposals

In other words, boilerplate proposals may provide an efficient means for communicating a seller's generic message, but they do little to document unique buyer applications or buyer-specific values needed for key account decision makers. Further, boilerplate proposals fail to identify buyer-specific improvement opportunities—the basis for any winning proposal.

For example, a large automobile fleet leasing company used a boilerplate approach to ensure that all their proposals were thorough and complete. In their proposals, the leasing company presented sophisticated systems and all the reasons a company would want to lease cars from them. To request a proposal from the home office, their sales representatives needed only to supply the prospective buyer's name. However, other than the buyer's name appearing wherever the word-processing system found the *[customer name]* field, their proposals represented little more than long, boring brochures. Their proposals forced buyers to:

- determine how the leasing company's services and systems might improve their operations and work in their unique environments and
- calculate how the leasing company's services would reduce vehicle acquisition and operating costs

This non-consultative selling behavior placed a tremendous burden on their buyers' decision-making processes.

Ironically, this leasing company had some of the best and most sophisticated fleet-leasing services available. However, they wanted their sales professionals to rely on relationship selling and vendor tactics rather than use a consultative sales process and strategic proposals. Their boilerplate proposals did not communicate value because they did not define a buyer-specific application and the resulting benefits. Rather, their proposals were so ineffective that buyers focused on price. It is not surprising that this leasing company closed less than 25 percent of their sales proposals. This meant competitors with lesser services and lower prices won 75 percent of the time—relationship selling was not sufficient to overcome a lower price.

"So What" Proposal

A proposal that does not present financial justification to the buyer can be classified as a "So What" proposal. After the buyer reads the proposal, he or she says, "So what? This seems like a good idea, but I just don't know what it will do for our bottom line." In most cases, the buyer is also saying that he or she does not have the time or does not know how to calculate the financial benefits of the proposed solution.

The "So What" proposal lacks the critical financial justifications that top management needs to make the buy decision. Writing this type of proposal puts the sale at risk because the buyer has no compelling reason to buy—top management has no financial information on which to make a decision. In some cases, the buyer may try to develop internal financial justifications to support the seller's proposal. But forcing the buyer into this situation is not very representative of a consultative selling or strategic proposal development. When this occurs, the seller loses control of the sale and credibility with the buyer. Successful sales professionals leave nothing to chance or miscalculation. They always control the proposal process and the numbers—the profit improvement analyses and calculations.

Buyer Assurances

Most buyers perceive risk when making a change. For example, a buyer will perceive risk when implementing a new system, hiring an unknown consulting firm, or installing a new piece of equipment. This risk weighs heavily in the buyer's decision process. To minimize risk, a strategic proposal presents pertinent information about the seller's competency and capabilities. The proposal helps assure the buyer that the seller can perform on the contract.

While working in the buyer-seller partnership, a sales professional can identify many of the buyer's concerns about the proposed change and make certain that the proposal adequately addresses each. For example, early in the sales process, a sales professional for a large software vendor learned that the buyer's last systems conversion was a disaster; it created tremendous customer service problems that took months to resolve. Obviously, converting to another new system presents great perceived risk for this buyer. The software vendor should use the strategic proposal to describe their conversion methods to assure the buyer that they will minimize business disruptions. The seller should include a detailed description of their conversion methodology in the proposal.

In some respects the proposal itself subliminally assures the buyer of the seller's capabilities. Besides thoroughly documenting the consultative sales process, such elements as format, paper quality, binding, and writing style can send strong messages about the selling organization's capabilities.

Basis for Future Opportunities

A seller's key account plans should contain an ongoing strategy for improving the buyer's profits or operations. Ideally, one strategic proposal will lead to follow-on opportunities, one improvement opportunity proposal flows out of a previous proposal and into a following proposal. The ongoing buyer-seller partnership forms the basis for future opportunities by providing critical knowledge about what to propose, to whom it should be proposed, and when to propose. The strategic proposal provides a consistent vehicle for presenting ongoing, profit improvement projects to the buyer's management.

For example, while writing their initial proposal for audit and tax services, a CPA firm would logically identify opportunities for providing additional services. These additional services might include new systems implementations, employee benefits administration, or strategic planning. After securing audit and tax engagements, the firm might logically propose implementation of a new accounts receivable system. Perhaps as the firm is implementing a new accounts receivable system, the engagement partner might propose cash management improvement opportunities to the client.

Business versus Technical Proposals

A sales proposal focuses primarily on business issues rather than technical issues, even though technical issues may be an integral component of many profit improvement opportunities. Technical aspects of the proposed solution should never overshadow the value of the proposed product's or service's profit or operations improvement opportunities. Top management is primarily interested in how much money the company will make or save or how much the operations will improve. Typically senior decision makers rely on their subordinates or buying committee representatives to evaluate technical feasibility and operational compatibility. Decision makers expect the seller's product or service application will work for their company or they would not be reviewing the proposal.

A proposal should contain only the technical information needed to support and justify the proposed business solutions. Technically-focused proposals usually fail because they do not address how the buyer will improve profits or operations even when they propose winning technologies. For example, a leading telecommunications company proposed that a regional telephone carrier replace its existing telephone lines with fiber-optic cables. This represented a huge investment and strategic business decision for the telephone company. The proposal was nearly two hundred pages long and did a spectacular job of presenting the company's leading-edge technology and its potential applications.

In reality, the proposal had little chance of winning. Even though the decision makers liked the technology, they declined the proposal. The seller failed to define the buyer-specific business improvement opportunities offered by the fiber optics technology. The proposal did little more than communicate technical information from the seller to the buyer.

Proposals that focus on technical issues often are symptomatic of several seller deficiencies:

- sales professionals lack the consultative skills needed to analyze the buyer's operation and present viable business improvement opportunities
- the seller's proposal team may have too many technocrats and too few business application specialists
- the seller may have a technological solution for which no viable business need exists

Readability Guidelines

A winning strategic proposal follows several guidelines to ensure readability. These guidelines form the basis for the recommended content and structure of a strategic proposal.

Sequence and Categorize Information

A proposal should present information using a logical flow of information and ideas. For example, a proposal should include a description of the custom application of the seller's proposed products or services followed by the resulting benefits. A proposal would be confusing if a main section contained background information on the buyer's improvement opportunity and the seller's proposed engagement schedule, not a logical grouping.

The proposal also must group information into interrelated, logical categories. For example, a main section presenting the seller's proposed solution should logically follow a section that defines the buyer's situation. It is inappropriate to present the seller's qualifications for performing on the contract before defining how the seller proposes to help the buyer realize their improvement opportunity.

Educate the Reader

Some decision makers have limited or no knowledge about a specific function or operation and the related profit improvement opportunities identified in the proposal. In these cases, the proposal must sufficiently educate the reader so that he or she can make an informed buying decision. The proposal team should write the proposal under the assumption that all recipients and decision makers have limited knowledge about the improvement opportunity.

For example, in a cross-functional buying committee comprised of division vice presidents, the Operations VP may not know how the company's automated human resource system works and would find it difficult to make an educated buying decision for a new system. Therefore, to educate this reader, the software vendor's proposal might graphically illustrate their system's hierarchical database structure, data requirements, and interrelationships with other internal buyer systems. This would help the Operations VP and probably other decision makers better understand their company's needs and the vendor's proposed software application.

Length

Many salespeople wonder about proposal length. Some of their most frequently asked questions are:

- What is the maximum acceptable proposal length?
- Should a $1 million proposal be longer than a $10,000 proposal?
- Will a buyer perceive a short proposal as deficient when compared to a longer one?

There are no right or wrong answers; however, there is some correlation between length and the complexity of the buyer's improvement opportunity and the seller's proposed solution. Certainly the cost of the proposed solution and/or the buyer's perceived risk may also affect length, although these factors are relative in each buying situation. Further, page format and type face size also affect length—a proposal printed in 10 point versus 12 point type would require fewer pages. Perhaps the best answer to the length question is, "Long enough to get a signed contract but short enough to hold the reader's attention."

The proposal team should consider two guidelines when writing a proposal:

- **Ask the buyer.** Some organizations may not accept lengthy proposals. They may expect that the main body of the proposal will be ten to fifteen pages long but have with no limits on appendices length.
- **Limit the amount of detail.** A well-written sales proposal will not bore the reader. Therefore, it should not include lengthy technical descriptions, product specifications, and/or activity or task lists in main sections. Rather, such information should be summarized and the supporting detail put in appendices.

Strategic Proposal Structure

This book's author bases the following strategic proposal structure on years of research and proposal evaluations for all types of businesses and industries.

Five Main Proposal Sections

A strategic proposal contains five main sections. These sections are interrelated and customer-focused. They categorize information and provide a logical sequence of information and ideas.

- **Background Information** identifies the buyer's current situation related strategy and the improvement opportunity—the buyer's unresolved problem or unachieved opportunity
- **Proposed Solution** presents the buyer-specific product or service application—how the seller can add value by helping the buyer achieve the improvement opportunity
- **Implementation Management** discusses the seller's methods for implementing the proposed product or service

- **Seller Profile** discusses the seller's qualifications and business practices
- **Business Issues** groups all business-related items for ease of review and reference, such as fees/prices, expenses, and invoicing schedule.

Chapters 4–8 provide detailed discussions of these five strategic proposal sections.

Proposal Components

Additionally, a strategic proposal should include the following components:

- **Title Page**
- **Executive Summary**—as its name implies, a concise synopsis of the entire proposal
- **Table of Contents**—a listing of main sections and subsections with page numbers
- **Appendices**—used to support information contained in the main proposal sections; a place for preprinted form, detailed financial calculations, product specifications, etc.

Chapter 9, "Important Proposal Components," discusses these proposal components in detail. The following diagram graphically illustrates the strategic proposal structure and components.

4. Section I: Background Information

Section Purpose

The first recommended main proposal section, *Background Information,* serves several purposes, it:

- documents the seller's in-depth understanding of the buyer's business organization, operations, and profit improvement strategies
- provides detailed background information, including key performance indicators, about the identified improvement opportunity
- defines the buyer's needs and objectives
- quantifies the buyer's improvement opportunity, the lower revenues or higher costs
- sets the stage for the seller's proposed solution

This first main proposal section must reflect the seller's empathy for the buyer. It must demonstrate a thorough understanding of the buyer's business, particularly the function or functions associated with the improvement opportunity. More important, the first main proposal section must document the findings of the buyer-seller partnership's improvement opportunity analyses. This must include the buyer's key performance indicators.

The first proposal section provides the reader with pertinent information about the improvement opportunity available to the buyer. It will become the knowledge foundation on which the decision makers will base their buying decision. To write this section, the seller needs to put himself in a decision maker's position. The sales professional should constantly ask one question when developing this section: *Does this section provide the reader with sufficient information about the function and the improvement opportunity on which to base an educated buying decision?*

For example, a CPA firm is proposing a $750,000 consulting engagement to improve a defense contractor's manufacturing process by reducing raw materials' inventory levels. How confident would one of the defense contractor's decision makers be in awarding the contract, if he or she does not thoroughly understand the current manufacturing process and the related problems facing the company? Some senior-level decision makers, particularly in large organizations, have little or no knowledge about some of their company's primary functions in which they are not directly involved. Therefore, a well-written proposal must educate its recipients to a level where they understand the improvement opportunity and feel confident about making a critical buying decision.

In this example, if the decision makers do not think the CPA firm totally understands their manufacturing problems, how confident would they be in awarding the $750,000 engagement contract? The answer to this question is obvious. In this situation, a non-empathetic proposal may reflect the CPA firm's inability or unwillingness to thoroughly analyze the buyer's situation. It may appear as though the CPA firm is arbitrarily proposing a major consulting engagement to correct a problem that they have not thoroughly analyzed. When decision makers do not think the seller really understands their unique improvement opportunity, they will also question the reliability of the seller's proposed solution. Further, when the buyer perceives the seller as non-empathetic, it greatly diminishes the probability of a favorable buying decision.

Typically when a proposal fails to adequately define the buyer's current situation or reflect the seller's understanding of the improvement opportunity, the buyer either (1) does not to make a buy decision or (2) delays buying until they can gather sufficient information on which to base a decision. A buying delay may represent a signal that the buyer wants more time to analyze the current situation. Delays often result in the seller losing any exclusivity that they may have had with the buyer. Chances are the buyer will start looking for competitive alternatives, which will only complicate the sale.

Therefore, the first proposal section is most critical to building a solid foundation for winning. It must educate the decision makers and build their confidence that the seller understands their business and the improvement opportunity. A well-written Background Information section effectively sets the stage for the seller's product or service offering.

Unbiased Analyses

The seller must take an unbiased approach in reporting the buyer's current situation. Above all, this proposal section needs to avoid any conflicts, criticism, or controversy that may arise from the analysis of the buyer's current situation, particularly if it reflects negatively on management's past decisions. It should represent an unbiased analysis of the buyer's current situation, not an exposé on poor management or past decisions. It should neither criticize the buyer's current operation nor display their lack of knowledge about available improvement opportunities options.

Typically, the sales professional will not know all the people in the buyer's organization who may influence the buying decision. For example, a decision maker's boss, subordinate, or close friend may be responsible for a current operational problem. Obviously, the proposal should not criticize someone's past management decisions. To do so could embarrass that person. It could make a decision maker defensive of the current situation and in opposition for the need to make a change. This also could result in resentment towards the seller, which certainly would put the sale at risk. Therefore, the seller should adhere to the *Joe Friday Approach—Just the Facts* when developing the first proposal section.

Section Titles

The seller may select a section title that more clearly defines the profit or operations improvement opportunity. For example, *Current Equipment Maintenance Program* or *Data Processing: Costs and Concerns*. Optionally, the section title might include the buyer's name. For example, *Current Equipment Maintenance Program: Acme Manufacturing* or *Data Processing Background Information for First National Bank*. The section title should help focus the readers' attention and thoughts.

Some alternative, more generic Section I titles include:

- Current Situation
- Present Operations
- Proposal Background
- Improvement Opportunity
- Statement of the Problem
- Statement of the Opportunity

Recommended Subsections

Section I reflects the seller's empathy for the buyer. It describes the buyer's current operation as it relates to the seller's proposed solution. The first main proposal section:

- defines the improvement opportunity—the unresolved problem or unachieved opportunity
- establishes current operations and costs or revenue levels
- lists the buyer's key performance indicators
- defines the buyer's *confirmed* needs and objectives

By definition, each key account buying situation is unique. Therefore, the seller should carefully decide what to include in this main section. Some recommended Section I subsections include:

- Industry Background
- Client/Customer Background
- Current Operations or Functions
- Improvement Opportunity [Definition, Analysis, and Plans]
- Client/Customer Needs and Objectives
- Purpose of This Proposal

Note: The seller might select subsection titles that more clearly describe their content. See the example Section I at the end of this chapter for example variations.

Industry Background

A well-crafted sales proposal educates its readers by providing key information. In certain situations the seller may choose to include an *Industry Information* subsection in the first section. The seller should consider using this optional subsection if the proposal recommends that the buyer implement a new service or manufacture a new product. This subsection will (1) help the buyer understand the market for the new product or service or (2) present a recent operational innovation in their industry. Industry background information gives proposal recipients a better understanding of current industry trends, innovators, and innovations as they relate to the buyer's unique situation. This section can also help position the seller as a recognized partner in the buyer's industry.

For example, if a paging software vendor is proposing that a paging company begin to offer alphanumeric paging services using their software, a strategic proposal might contain a subsection about the rapidly growing alphanumeric paging business. This subsection could include information about alphanumeric paging: history, major service providers, types of applications, growth projections, and the number and demographics of alphanumeric subscribers. Further, this subsection could identify recent applications of the seller's software. This background information will educate the paging company decision makers about the new business opportunity being proposed by paging software vendor.

Client or Customer Background

This subsection provides a brief overview of the buyer's business. It should include *general* buyer information, such as number of employees, annual revenues, number, and number of locations to assure the buyer that the seller understands their business. More importantly, this subsection should include detailed buyer information that is relevant to the seller's proposed solution. For example, if the seller is proposing an employee profit-sharing program, then this section would include employee age and demographic information. This educates the decision makers by giving them information about how many of the company's employees are eligible to participate in the program— information needed to make a buying decision.

Current Operations or Functions

The proposal must define the buyer's current operations or functions as they relate to the specific improvement opportunity under analysis. This subsection often educates those decision makers who have limited knowledge about complex functions in a large organization. Remember, a winning sales proposal must provide sufficient information for the decision makers to make an educated decision. If the decision makers find it difficult to understand the improvement opportunity facing the company, they also will find it difficult to buy the seller's proposed solution.

For example, if the seller is proposing the implementation of an advanced machinery maintenance program, then this subsection should include information about the buyer's machines: numbers and types, current maintenance policies and procedures, average downtimes, and number of maintenance staff. It should provide sufficient information so all decision makers can become more knowledgeable about their company's machinery maintenance challenges.

Improvement Opportunity (Definition, Analysis, and Plans)

A winning sales proposal *sets the stage* for the seller's solution. To do so, it first must concisely define the buyer's improvement opportunity, and the resulting costs incurred or the revenues missed. This may seem like a straightforward concept; however, the buyer and seller must agree on the existence and definition of the improvement opportunity, including financial measurements. The seller cannot fabricate a buyer improvement opportunity just to make a sale; this would nullify the trust and confidence within the buyer-seller partnership and destroy the seller's credibility.

The *Improvement Opportunity* subsection includes the observed causes of the problem or opportunity including a brief discussion of their financial impact. This discussion defines how the buyer measures the financial impact and contains actual calculations. The specific financial measures defined in this section will be the basis for measuring the financial benefits of the seller's proposed solution. In other words, they *set the stage* for the next main proposal section, which presents the seller's product or service.

For example, First National Bank (FNB) buys data processing services from a service bureau and spends 20 percent more than its peer group banks for these services. Annually, data processing services cost FNB $350,000. This represents 18 percent of the bank's *Other Expenses* and equates to $0.043 *Earnings per Share,* these measures represent *Key Performance Indicators* for FNB. When a bank systems vendor proposed an in-house system, they measured the financial benefits of their proposed systems based on the bank's Key Performance Indicators: *Other Expenses* and *Earnings per Share* measures. They included the current financial measures in the first section and used these measures in the second section to calculate financial benefits of their proposed solution.

By using these Key Performance Indicators in the first and second proposal sections, the vendor provided FNB's decision makers with the information they needed to evaluate *value*. Their proposal provided the cost-benefit analysis information based on the bank's unique situation. It represented the information the bank's decision makers needed to confidently make an informed buy decision.

Further, if the buyer has plans for achieving the improvement opportunity, then the team should describe them in the proposal. Optionally, this subsection might discuss an ongoing project the buyer has in place to address the improvement opportunity.

Some examples:

- First National Bank established a committee to evaluate the viability of converting to an in-house system as a means of reducing its data processing costs.
- To gain better control of its inventory process, Acme Manufacturing started a project to standardize inventory item numbers in its three recently acquired warehouses.

The *Improvement Opportunity* subsection provides an excellent chance to present the seller's proactive sales process to the decision makers. To secure a signed contract in most key account situations, the seller's proposed solution must complement the buyer's improvement strategies. Ideally, the proposal will help the decision makers view the seller's proposed products or services as an integral component of their strategies. If the seller's proposed products or services fits the buyer's strategies, then the buyer often takes *ownership* of the proposed solution. The buyer may even view the seller's proposed solution as their idea. If this *ownership* attitude permeates to the decision makers, it greatly increases the seller's probability for securing a signed contract.

Needs and Objectives

To *set the stage* for the seller's proposed product or service, the first proposal section must clearly identify the buyer's *confirmed* needs and objectives. Decision makers are very likely to make a buying decision when the seller's proposed solution satisfies their organization's needs and objectives. This does not mean the strategic proposal process is manipulative. Rather, it reflects the seller's customer-driven, consultative sales approach. When a sales professional understands and confirms the key account's needs and objectives as they relate to their strategies, he or she can use this knowledge to develop a custom application for the buyer. It is the seller's custom application that becomes the basis for converting product features or service capabilities into buyer-specific benefits—adding value.

For example, an affluent client is too busy to properly manage her $750,000 investment portfolio that is held in three brokerage accounts. Last year's total return, her Key Performance Indicator, on her portfolio was only $28,900, less than 4.0 percent. This affluent client needs professional investment management expertise and service. A trust company sales professional will identify and confirm these needs with the client before proposing a change. By listing the client's needs in the first proposal section, the sales professional *sets the stage* for the trust company's services, which will be described in Section II: *Proposed Solution.*

This second section must discuss how a trust arrangement would result in consolidated record keeping, improved performance, and consistent investment advice—the benefits that satisfied the client's specific needs. The custom application will help convince this client that the trust company clearly understands her needs and is uniquely qualified to provide her with custom, personalized services.

Purpose of This Proposal

The last recommended subsection in the first main proposal section serves as a transition to the second main section, *Proposed Solution.* This subsection recaps the key points of the first section and introduces the seller's proposed product or service. Some salespeople feel it unnecessary to include this subsection. They think if the first section adequately defines the buyer's profit or operations improvement opportunity, then it should be obvious to the reader what and why the seller is proposing. While this is a valid position, a sales professional should never overlook the need to ensure buyer focus. This is especially true if any of the buyer's decision makers have limited knowledge about the operation affected by the unresolved problem or unachieved opportunity.

For example, an employee selection testing company that proposed its services to an insurance company used the following *Purpose of This Proposal* subsection. This example recaps Star Insurance Company's needs and wants, e.g., lower interview costs, reduce turnover, etc., and takes the reader to the next section.

SelecTest's proposal to Star Insurance Company has two purposes. It will first show how its Employee Selection Testing System [ESTS] can:

- *reduce interview costs*
- *improve the quality of new hires*
- *reduce job-employee mismatches*
- *reduce employee turnover*

Next, this proposal will present SelecTest's proposed implementation of ESTS at Star Insurance Company and its resulting nonfinancial and financial benefits.

Design and Development Checklist

Complete these tasks to design and develop the first section of the strategic proposal, Background Information:

1. **Select an appropriate name for the section.** The title "Background Information" is generic. Adding the prospect's name to the title makes the proposal more custom, i.e., ABC Manufacturing Background Information. However, a custom section title means custom tab dividers.
2. **Select and review the subsections to include in the first section.** The recommended subsections are:
   - Industry Background (optional)
   - Client/Customer Background
   - Current Operations or Functions
   - Improvement Opportunity
   - Client/Customer Needs and Objectives
   - Purpose of This Proposal
3. **Decide what to include in the "Industry Background" subsection, if used.** If the proposal will have an Industry Background subsection, decide what industry information to include. Remember, this subsection should help educate the reader about the directions and trends in the industry that cre-

ate opportunities for the buyer. The proposed product or service should help the buyer realize the opportunities.

4. **Decide how to title and what customer information to include in the "Client or Customer Background" subsection.** The first subsection must demonstrate the seller's understanding of the buyer. It might include such client information as business description, annual revenues, number of locations, etc. If the section title is generic, this subsection might include the client's name, e.g., XYZ Data Services Profile.

5. **Decide how to title and what pertinent information to include in the "Current Operations or Functions" subsection.** This subsection defines the buyer's current operations or functions as they relate to the specific improvement opportunity discussed in the next subsection. It must provide sufficient information to make an educated buying decision. A custom subsection title might help the reader focus and understand, e.g., New Employee Selection Process.

6. **Decide how to title and what to include in the "Improvement Opportunity" subsection.** Use this subsection to clearly define the business improvement opportunity available; the proposed product or service will help the buyer capitalize on the opportunity. This subsection also should include a thorough analysis of the opportunity and any plans the client might have for taking advantage of it. A custom subsection title might include the buyer's name, e.g., First National Bank—Internet Banking Opportunities.

7. **Decide how to title and what to include in the "Client Needs and Objectives" subsection.** This subsection should summarize the previous two subsections by clearly defining the client's needs and objectives as they relate to the buyer's business and improvement opportunity and the seller's proposed product or service. A custom title would include the buyer's name and/or the name of the affected business operation or function, e.g., Fleet Identification Program Needs and Objectives.

8. **Decide what to include in the "Purpose of This Proposal" subsection.** Use this subsection as a transition to the next main section, Proposed Solution, and to help define the buyer's expectations for the proposal. Include statements about what the proposed product or service will do for the buyer, e.g., show

how ABC Graphics can reduce production costs through the use of digital imaging. Also introduce the seller's implementation methodology or practices.

Section I Example

The following Section I example is:

- to Pacific Food Systems, a food distribution company
- from National Institute for Drug Prevention, a company selling its workplace substance abuse deterrence and detection system.

I. Company Background: PFS

Our Understanding of PFS. Pacific Food Systems, PFS, a wholly-owned subsidiary of Pacific Enterprises, Inc., provides food distribution services to independent restaurants. PFS:

- has 2,500 associates
- services 14,000 restaurant customers
- had revenues over $2.8 billion in 1997; the result of
    - delivering 3.3 million pounds of products
    - traveling 38 million delivery miles
    - making 1.4 million deliveries
- has distribution points scattered throughout the western U.S.

William F. Fisher, PFS President, stated in the annual report:

The words, change, innovation, and growth describe the dynamics and challenging environment in which PFS operates. In a year characterized by constant challenges, we never faltered in our push to create productivity, while we grew our business by more than 15 percent to $2.8 billion, serviced more than 14,000 restaurant customers, while reducing 3.5 million miles from our service routes.

This shows evidence of a dynamic company, searching for ways to improve.

Substance Abuse at PFS. Measuring the magnitude and cost of alcohol or other drug (AOD) abuse is an easy calculation, assuming PFS's workplace demographics follow

- average percent of employees who are substance abusers: 10 percent
- annual employer cost for each substance abuser: $10,000
- PFS Associates who are substance abusers: 250
- Estimated annual substance abuse cost for PFS: $2,500,000.

Again, assuming PFS's demographics reflect national averages, the distribution of associates who abuse alcohol versus other drugs is 64 percent to 36 percent. This provides an estimate of substance abusers by type:

- alcohol abusers: 160
- illicit drug abusers: 90

PFS Drug-Free Workplace Programs. PFS realizes the devastating effect AOD abuse has on American business. To combat substance abuse and provide a drug-free workplace for its associates, PFS currently uses five programs.

- Pre-employment Testing
- Just Cause Testing
- Random Testing
- Post-accident Testing
- Employee Assistance Program

Pre-employment Testing Program. PFS gives each job applicant a urinalysis test before offering them an associate's position. An analysis of PFS's Pre-employment Testing Program for 1997 provides the following information:

· number of tests	646
· cost per test	$35
· total program cost	$22,610
· positive test rate	2.2%
· total positive tests	14
· cost to detect a drug abuser applicant	$1,579

Further analysis of the Pre-employment Testing Program based upon published AOD statistics indicates (1) 10 percent or 65 of PFS's 646 job applicants will be AOD abusers and (2) AOD abusers are typically divided as follows: 64 percent alcohol and 36 percent drugs. Therefore:

- 36 percent or 23 PFS applicants abused drugs and nine (9) applicants "cleaned-up" long enough to pass PFS's Pre-employment tests; the remaining 14 applicants who were drug abusers tested positive
- the remaining 42 AOD abusers evaded detection since urinalysis testing does not detect alcohol abuse

Just Cause Testing. PFS's managers and supervisors may request a bodily fluid test for an associate whose job performance provides *just cause* to suspect impairment in the workplace. In 1996, five (5) bodily fluid tests were requested as the result of this program. Note: An effective just cause testing program requires managers and supervisors to have the knowledge and skills needed to identify and handle impairment situations.

Random Drug Testing. PFS has a random drug testing program. During 1996, 135 tests were given at a cost of $4,725. The positive rate was 6 percent, far above the national average of 1 percent. From previous statistical data, PFS can expect positive test rates from its Random Drug Testing Program to range from less than 1.0 percent (0.8 percent) to nearly 3.0 percent. During 1996, Department of Transportation [DOT] mandated random tests were performed. By DOT mandate, 50 percent of DOT regulated employees must be tested annually. PFS tested 957 employees subject to DOT regulations. Program costs were $33,495.

PFS received some negative reactions from its Random Drug Testing program. Many organizations that voluntarily or involuntarily implemented a Random Drug Testing Program experienced adverse employee responses:

- Some of the 90 percent of their employees, who are not drug abusers, resented the invasiveness of urinalysis testing. They felt the tests invaded their privacy and did not respect their dignity.
- Some employees, who use marijuana away from the workplace, tested positive because traces of this illicit drug can stay in the body for up to three weeks. These employees claimed they were

not impaired at the workplace and therefore challenged the resulting disciplinary action.

Additionally, employers have found that a Random Drug Testing Program did nothing to deter alcohol abuse in the workplace.

Post-accident Testing. In 1996, PFS managers and supervisors reported 626 lost time injury accidents. The post- accident test showed a 10 percent positive test rate at a cost of $21,910 (626 urinalysis tests at $35 per test). Typically, the number of accidents rises proportionally with the number of employees. If PFS continues each year to increase the number of associates by 10 percent, then the number of accidents and post- accident bodily fluid testing will be as follows:

Year	Est. # of Accidents	Est. Testing Cost
1997	688	$24,080
1998	756	$26,460

A Post-accident Testing Program:

- will limit PFS's liability to the involved associate if drug impairment was a contributing cause of the accident
- will not limit PFS's liability to third parties or other associates injured by the acts or omissions of an impaired associate

NOTE: Typically, accidents requiring hospitalization will include blood tests administered at the hospital. These blood tests will determine the presence and level of AOD.

Employee Assistance Program. PFS provides its associates with an Employee Assistance Program (EAP). The EAP is externally staffed, under contract. Annual cost of this program is $50,000.

Summary of 1996 PFS Substance Abuse Program Costs

- AOD Substance abuse (250 x $10,000) $2,500,000
- Pre-employment Testing $22,610
- Just Cause Testing $175
- Random Testing $33,495
- Post-accident Testing $21,910
- Employee Assistance Program $50,000

Total $2,628,190

PFS Substance Abuse Program Needs and Objectives. After careful review of their current drug-free workplace programs, PFS needs to find a more cost-effective solution to substance abuse. Specifically, PFS's objective is to implement a program that:

- addresses alcohol and drug abuse (not only drugs)
- reduces or eliminates the need to administer pre-employment testing of prospective new hires
- enhances the use of just cause and post-accident testing
- eliminates the need to use random drug testing except when mandated by the DOT
- complements their current Employee Assistance Program

Purpose of this Proposal. The purpose of this proposal is twofold:

- present PFS with the National Institute on Drug Prevention's *AOD Alert System,* an integrated system for substance abuse detection and deterrence
- show how the *AOD Alert System* will help PFS control AOD costs through the use of a noninvasive screening process

5. Section II: Proposed Business Solution

Section Purpose

The second of five recommended main proposal sections, *Proposed Business Solution,* serves several purposes, it:

- describes the seller's proposed solution, the proposed product or service that will help the buyer achieve the improvement opportunity
- defines how the proposed product or service will operate within the buyer's unique environment—the custom application
- presents the proposed product's or service's features and the non-financial benefits provided to the buyer—*soft value*
- presents the financial benefits that the buyer will receive as a direct result of implementing the proposed solution—*hard value*
- helps differentiate the seller because it epitomizes their customer-driven, consultative sales approach

This second section must provide the buyer's decision makers with a clear understanding of the seller's proposed solution and describe how it will help achieve the profit improvement opportunities identified in the first section. It must also demonstrate the seller's ability to define a realistic application for their proposed product or service to fit in the buyer's business. Further, this section must present the decision makers with compelling reasons to make a change.

Perhaps, the second proposal section offers the greatest development challenges for the sales professional and the greatest opportunities for seller differentiation. In a consultative, sales process, the proposal cannot simply present generic product or service descriptions. Rather, the sales professional must first define a buyer-specific application. The more clearly the seller defines the application in terms of the buyer's unique situation, then the easier it becomes for the decision makers to make a buying decision. The buying decision is easier because the proposal helps them to understand how the product or service will work for their company. It is the documentation of this aspect of the consultative sales process that helps the decision makers differentiate the seller.

Therefore, the more a sales professional can define a viable application for the buyer, the more he or she can differentiate themselves from the competition. For example, a trust company can offer a variety of sophisticated, personal trust products and services to its affluent clients. A winning proposal would not simply include a generic description for one of these products that leaves the client to decide how it might apply to her situation. Rather, the sales professional would define the proposed trust product application based upon the client's unique personal circumstances. The proposal defines the application.

By defining a buyer-specific application for the proposed product or service, the seller builds the foundation for developing buyer-specific nonfinancial and financial benefits— value. To improve the probability of getting a sale, the team must convert product features and/or service capabilities into customer-specific value. Like the clearly defined application, buyer-specific benefits differentiate the seller.

For example, generic product or service benefits statements such as "automated document assembly can save your staff valuable time," have little meaning to decision makers who don't understand which company documents need to be automated and how automating their assembly can save time. Rather, a winning sales proposal will define which buyer documents will be automated and include buyer-specific accuracy improvement and cost-reduction calculations. Certainly, this type of proposal will educate the decision makers and differentiate the seller that developed it.

A strong *Section II: Proposed Business Solution* is dependent on a strong first proposal section. A sales professional understands that thorough buyer analysis makes the difference between winning and losing. Inadequate analysis leads to poor application definition, which makes it difficult to define buyer-specific values. Therefore, three elements represent the critical components of a winning strategic sales proposal:

- a thorough understanding of the buyer's improvement opportunity,
- a clearly defined, custom application, and
- fully developed buyer-specific values.

These three elements also define the most common shortcomings of *So What* and *Boilerplate* proposals.

Link Needs and Objectives to Solutions

The previous chapter presents the concept that the first proposal section *sets the stage* for the second section by defining the buyer's needs and objectives. When a selling organization defines the custom application, they must link the buyer's needs and objectives to the proposed product or service. This links the buyer's improvement opportunity to the seller's products or services.

For example, *Acme Manufacturing Company* employs 150 people and experiences payroll processing problems. The company has outgrown its current system, an improvement opportunity, which results in the following needs and objectives:

- lower processing costs
- integration with the company's job reporting system
- comprehensive regulatory reporting
- direct deposit of payroll checks

Acme expects to outsource its processing to a firm specializing in payroll services. Acme wants the payroll processor to allow its payroll clerk to submit data and information using an on-line terminal or terminal emulator—another objective. Therefore, when *Electronic Payroll Services (EPS),* a payroll processor, presents a proposal that satisfies Acme's needs and objectives, the probability of securing a signed contract increases. Key to EPS's success will be their ability to clearly identify Acme's improvement opportunity and the related needs and objectives. Next EPS must link these needs and objectives to their payroll service's capabilities and corresponding benefits. The more EPS is able to define their proposed service and its application in Acme-specific terms, the more they differentiate their services and themselves, and the higher the probability for obtaining a signed contract.

This linkage process sounds logical and easy. However, one of the greatest challenges in most complex sales situations lies in clearly defining the buyer's improvement opportunity, establishing valid buyer needs and objectives, and then presenting a realistic application of the seller's proposed solution in the buyer's business environment. Therefore, the second proposal section creates the critical linkage between the buyer and the seller—a well-defined improvement opportunity linked to a realistic application equates to seller differentiation and more closed sales.

Section Titles

Alternative titles would include the name of the proposed products or services or describe the proposed solution. For example, a trust company might title the second section *Proposed Personal Trust Services.* A software company might use the name of their proposed system in the section title, e.g., *Proposed PowerMfg System.* Alternative generic section titles include:

- Proposed Services
- Proposed Project
- Proposed Improvement Project
- Proposed Consulting Engagement
- Proposed Strategy

Recommended Subsections

Section II of a strategic proposal should contain four recommended subsections:

- Product or Service Description
- Product or Service Application
- Nonfinancial (Qualitative) Benefits
- Financial (Quantitative) Benefits

The seller may select subsection titles that include the name of the proposed product or service. For example, a company that sells environmental systems for buildings might title their subsections as follows:

- *EnviroControl III Description*
- *EnviroControl III for Comstock Property Management*
- *EnviroControl III Nonfinancial Benefits*
- *EnviroControl III Financial Benefits*

Product or Service Description

The first Section II subsection presents the seller's proposed products or services. It should briefly describe the products or services, including their operating specifications, capacities, service levels, service frequency, deliverables, etc.

Product or Service Application

The second subsection defines how the seller will apply the products or services in the buyer's business or operation. Generally, the proposed solution's complexity is directly proportional to this subsection's length. While writing it, the seller should keep in mind that this is a business proposal, not a technical proposal. He or she should ensure that the technical content of this subsection does not overshadow the business aspects of the proposed solution. Where possible, the subsection should include summaries of technical information and use supporting appendices for the detail. The sales professional should remember that most decision makers have more interest in the potential business improvement opportunities or benefits than in the technical details of the solution. In most situations, decision makers will assume the proposed product or service will work. But they really want to know how it will maximize their company's improvement opportunity.

The application subsection must specifically define how the proposed solution will operate or be provided in the buyer's unique environment. During the sales and proposal development process, the buyer-seller partnership should carefully evaluate all aspects of the application. This subsection should include the pertinent application information from their analysis. By doing so, the proposal helps assure the decision makers that the team has investigated application issues and considerations. It also will help minimize the decision makers' concerns regarding the appropriateness and viability of the purchase decision.

A sales proposal that does not define the proposed product or service application leaves the buyer without the critical information needed to make an informed buying decision. *Boilerplate* or *So What* proposals represent these nonconsultative sales and proposal processes. These proposal types attempt to treat all buyers the same—generic application of products or services. This forces a buyer to define the application for their company, a totally ineffective sales process. Further, not all buyers will take the time needed to define the application, especially for the products or services in most complex sales. Obviously a *Boilerplate* or *So What* proposal jeopardizes the sale because it (1) does not document a buyer-specific application of the seller's products or services and (2) sends the wrong message about the selling organization.

For example, when *AutoLease,* an automobile fleet leasing company, proposed that *VendAll,* a nationwide vending machine company, implement a fleet leasing program for its vehicles, the proposal included specific application information:

- who at *VendAll* would get periodic vehicle maintenance reports and how they would use the reports' information
- how a *VendAll* vehicle user would obtain periodic preventative maintenance from local service providers across the country
- what options *VendAll* could offer their employees who might want to buy their vehicle at the end of the lease term

Certainly, this type of application information helped *VendAll*'s management make an informed buying decision and helped differentiate *AutoLease.*

Two Benefit Types

A strategic proposal should define two benefit types for the buyer: nonfinancial and financial. The two types are defined as follows:

Nonfinancial / Qualitative. Of, relating to, or concerning quality of the proposed product or service. It is difficult for the buyer and seller to measure these benefits in financial terms; therefore, they represent *soft value.*

Financial / Quantitative. Of, relating to, or susceptible of measurement—the monetary improvements provided by the proposed solution. These benefits measure financial impact for the buyer and represent *hard value.*

The relevance of a proposal's nonfinancial and financial benefits and their effectiveness in favorably persuading the decision makers, is dependent upon how well the buyer-seller partnership have completed two sales activities: (1) identifying the buyer's Key Performance Indicators, needs, and objectives and (2) defining how the proposed products or services would apply to the buyer's unique environment. These are consultative, customer-driven sales activities and typically present the greatest challenges in most complex sales situations.

This book integrates consultative selling and proposal development processes, and supports the need for in-depth customer analysis as the foundation for selling and developing strategic proposals. There are no substitutes for in-depth buyer knowledge and a solid grounding in product or service application. Logic follows that the more the seller knows about the buyer's operation, the easier it will be to define a concise application, and the easier it will be to develop specific buyer benefits.

For example, *FastPRNT,* a printing and duplication company, wanted to provide outsourcing services to *Andrews University,* a private university. To develop realistic nonfinancial and financial benefits, *FastPRNT*'s proposal team analyzed the university's printing and duplication functions including: costs, staffing and equipment, job types, volumes, and future projections. The team also identified the university's needs and objectives. Of course these were the analysis activities needed to write the first proposal section, *Background Information.* Once *FastPRNT*'s proposal team understood *Andrews*'s situation, they easily formulated a unique outsourcing service plan. The plan represented a custom application of *FastPRNT*'s services. It presented compelling reasons for the university to outsource its printing and duplication services. Developing the custom application helped *FastPRNT* identify custom benefits for *Andrews;* only benefits *FastPRNT* could provide.

Nonfinancial (Qualitative) Benefits

The Nonfinancial or Qualitative Benefits subsection identifies the *soft value adding* aspects of the proposed solution. These are the benefits that do not easily lend themselves to financial measure. They represent the *soft value* provided by the proposed solution. The buyer-seller partnership defines custom nonfinancial benefits by converting the proposed product's features and/or service's capabilities into buyer benefits. This reinforces the notion that the partnership must (1) understand the customer's improvement opportunities and (2) develop a buyer-specific application before defining nonfinancial benefits. Without a good understanding of the buyer's situation and a custom application definition a strategic proposal quickly becomes a *Boilerplate* or *So What* proposal.

To facilitate the *Feature-Benefit* (or *Capability-Benefit*) *Conversion* process, a proposal team might use the following process:

- Make three columns titled: Product Feature or Service Capability, Generic Benefit, and Customer-Specific Benefit or Value.
- List the proposed product features or service features.
- For each feature or capability, identify one or more resulting generic benefits. Note: Generic benefits are those benefits that all buyers generally will realize.
- For each generic benefit, develop a customer-specific benefit or value that only the buyer will realize from the application of the product or service in their unique environment.

For example, *BDP,* a software company, sells turnkey data processing systems to small- to medium-sized financial institutions. *BDP* developed the following qualitative benefits for *First State National Bank:*

Feature	Generic Benefit	Customer-Specific Benefit
Open systems architecture	high performance / low equipment cost	ability to replace the two outdated XM34 mid-range CPUs that require proprietary operating systems
Integrated office automation tools	every workstation has access to word processing, spreadsheet, database, and electronic mail	eliminate the need to have a terminal and PC on each Personal Banker's desk.

These custom benefits could only relate to *First State National Bank*'s unique situation. The *BDP* sales professional, or more correctly the buyer-seller partnership, could not have developed these buyer-specific qualitative benefits if they did not have (1) an in-depth knowledge of the bank's current situation and (2) a concise understanding of the proposed *BDP* system's application.

Financial (Quantitative) Benefits

The Financial or Quantitative Benefits subsection defines the reduced costs or increased revenues the buyer receives by implementing the proposed product or service, the proposal's *hard value.* This subsection demonstrates the financial viability of the seller's proposed solution and how it supports the buyer's profit improvement strategies. These benefits must be realistic and supported by unquestionable financial analyses. Again, this subsection is dependent on the *Background Information* section, which includes a definition of the buyer's improvement opportunity and measurements of the buyer's potential cost reductions or revenue enhancements. Logically, this second section uses buyer-defined Key Performance Indicators as a basis for calculating the proposed solution's financial impact. This gives the decision makers a valid means to judge the *hard value* of the seller's proposed product or service. In other words, the financial measures used to calculate the buyer's current costs or missed revenues in Section I are the same financial measures used in Section II. Using consistent financial measures provides the decision makers with valid information on which to make a decision.

For example, *Acme Services Corporation (ASC)* had a 55 percent annual turnover rate within its 300 customer services representatives (CSRs); this was 35 percent above the national average for similar businesses. Over the past several years, high turnover had eroded service levels and created numerous customer service problems. *Precision Staffing Systems (PSS),* a company that develops employee profile testing systems, and *ASC* representatives completed an extensive analysis of the situation. Their buyer-seller partnership determined that 50 percent of the turnover problems were attributable to employee- job mismatches. This meant 82 of the 165 new employees hired each year were not well suited for their positions.

Next, the *ASC* and *PSS* team calculated CSR turnover costs:

• Recruiting and hiring costs	$1,500
• CSR training costs	$2,000
• Number of new CSRs per year	165
• Total annual new CSR costs	$577,500
• Total annual new CSR costs attributed to mismatches (82 x [1,500 + 2,000])	$287,000

This analysis and the resulting financial measures gave *PSS* an ideal opportunity to develop the following financial benefits that cost-justified the implementation of their testing service at ASC. Using past experiences with similar clients, *PSS* estimated that their employee profiling system

52

would reduce ASC's CSR employee-job mismatches by 90 percent. *PSS* licenses its employee profiling systems for $95,000 and charges 15 percent ($14,250) annual maintenance fees after the first year. Additionally, *PSS* charged *ASC* $20,000 to customize the system. *ASC* implementation costs totaled $105,000. The buyer-seller partnership calculated financial benefits as follows:

• New CSR recruiting, hiring and training costs	$3,500
• Number of CSR mismatches each year	82
• Number of CSR mismatches eliminated through PSS's employee profiling system (90 percent x 82)	74
• 1st year ASC Gross Cost Savings	$259,000
• 1st year PSS fees	$105,000
• 1st year ASC net cost savings	$154,000
• ASC payback period	.68 years

This financial or quantitative benefits analysis presented *ASC*'s decision makers with *PSS*'s hard value and expedited their favorable buying decision. Certainly the two Key Performance Indicators, cost savings and payback period, made the decision easy.

A strategic proposal must match financial benefits to how the buyer calculates the costs or unachieved revenues associated with the improvement opportunity. Further, the buyer-seller partnership should: (1) use generally accepted financial calculations to measure the benefits and (2) use the financial calculations normally used by the buyer to make key buying decisions—the buyer's Key Performance Indicators. Some generally accepted financial calculations include:

Return On Investment (ROI)

Return on Investment, or ROI, is the most common investment performance measure, which is calculated as follows:

$$\text{Return on Investment} = \frac{\text{Income}}{\text{Invested Capital}}$$

Payback Method

The period of time needed for the after-tax cash inflows from the project to accumulate to an amount equal to the invested capital is the Payback Method.

$$\text{Payback Period} = \frac{\text{Invested Capital}}{\text{Annual After-tax Cash Inflow}}$$

Net Present Value (NPV)

To calculate Net Present Value, follow these steps:

1. Identify the cash flows for each year of the proposed investment.
2. Using a discount rate, calculate the present value of each cash flow.
3. The sum of the present values is the Net Present Value.
4. The buyer will favorably consider the proposed investment if the NPV is positive.

Earnings Per Share (EPS)

Many senior managers are also investors in common stock of their company. They hope to earn a return on their investment from dividends and increases in the stock price, two things that are closely related to the company's ability to earn income. Earnings Per Share is a key measure that relates a company's earnings to its common stock.

$$\text{Earnings Per Share} = \frac{\text{net income available to common shareholders}}{\text{weighted average number of shares of outstanding common stock}}$$

Accounting Rate of Return (ARR) Method

Accounting income is based on accrual accounting procedures. The incremental accounting income that results from the proposed project is the focus of the Accounting Rate of Return Method; revenue and expenses

54

are recognized during the period sold or incurred, not when cash is actually received or paid.

$$ARR = \frac{\text{average incremental income} - \text{average incremental expenses}}{\text{initial investment}}$$

*including depreciation and income taxes

Design and Development Checklist

Complete these tasks to design and develop the second section of the strategic proposal, Proposed Solution:

1. **Select an appropriate name for the section.** The title "Proposed Solution" is generic. Adding the seller's name or identifying the proposed product or service makes the proposal more custom, e.g., ABC Graphics Proposed Solution, Proposed Cash Management Services, Proposed Consulting Services.
2. **Review the four recommended subsections to include in the section.**
   - Product or Service Description
   - Product or Service Application
   - Nonfinancial Benefits
   - Financial Benefits
3. **Decide how to title and what to include in the "Product or Service Description" subsection.** The product or service name might make a good title for this subsection, e.g., PowerBank Cash Management System, AutoPhone Interactive Processing Services, or Audit Services. Develop a high-level overview of the proposed product or service by presenting major functions and listing major components.
4. **Decide how to title and what to include in the "Product or Service Application" subsection.** This critical subsection must describe how the proposed product or service will work in the buyer's business environment. A custom subsection title will help position the reader, e.g., PowerBank Cash Management System for First National Bank, AutoPhone Interactive Call Processing for Precision Mail Order, or Audit Services for ABC Manufacturing. Use this subsection to link major product

components or service capabilities to the buyer. For example, if a proposed service component is just-in-time delivery of a raw material, describe how the seller will coordinate material quantities and delivery times with the buyer's production systems.

5. **Decide how to title and what to include in the "Nonfinancial Benefits" subsection.** The title "Nonfinancial Benefits" clearly describes this subsection's content; however, adding a product or service identifier may be helpful, e.g., Nonfinancial Benefits—AutoPhone Interactive Call Processing. List product features or service capabilities along with their generic benefits and resulting buyer-specific benefits.

6. **Decide how to title and what to include in the "Financial Benefits" subsection.** The title "Financial Benefits" certainly describes subsection content. However, a benefit-specific title or a title containing a product or service identifier can be quite effective, e.g., Reduced Shipping Costs with Amalgamated Parcel Service. Include a comprehensive cost analysis using buyer-specific numbers. When developing this subsection, put yourself on the buyer's side of the desk and try to cost-justify the product or service.

Section II Example

The following example Section II is:

- to USA Logistics, a medium-size trucking company headquartered in Dallas, Texas
- from Advanced Wireless Concepts, Inc., a telecommunications systems integrator

II. Proposed Wireless Communications Solutions

To meet their driver communications needs and freight revenue objectives, Advanced Wireless Concepts (AWC) proposes USA Logistics (USAL) integrate three wireless communications system components:

1. cellular telephones
2. mobile facsimile machines
3. alphanumeric pagers

Wireless Systems Application for USA Logistics. AWC will install a cellular telephone and mobile facsimile machine in each truck and provide each driver with an alphanumeric pager.

Cellular Telephone Application. An in-truck cellular telephone will serve two primary purposes:

- a device for dialing telephone numbers for the fax machine
- an *emergency only* in-truck telephone for drivers

The cellular telephone will only allow calls to preprogrammed numbers to avoid nonbusiness use by the drivers. Preprogrammed numbers would include: USAL Dispatch and terminals, 911, etc.

Mobile Facsimile Application. An in-truck mobile, not portable, fax machine serves one primary purpose: provides a USAL driver with the ability to fax Bill of Lading and other related shipping documents to Dispatch. However, some key secondary uses include the ability for:

- USAL Dispatch to fax schedule changes, directions, and detailed maps to a driver
- a USAL driver to fax daily location and status reports to Dispatch

See Appendix C for cellular telephone and mobile facsimile machine technical specifications. See Appendix D for equipment installation options.

Alphanumeric Pagers Applications. The alphanumeric pagers provide a low-cost communications media for sending meaningful messages to drivers. The proposed pagers would offer statewide (Texas) or national coverage, as needed. USAL Dispatch could send multiple, 80-character messages to drivers using a standard, IBM compatible personal computer equipped with a modem.

See Appendix E for alphanumeric pager and paging software technical specifications.

Non-Financial Benefits

Wireless Component	Features	Benefits and Value to USAL
Cellular Telephone	Preprogrammed numbers	• drivers can only make calls to numbers preprogrammed into the telephone • no personal use by drivers
	Wireless emergency communications	• improved driver safety; drivers can call in the event of an equipment breakdown or severe weather conditions • drivers do not have to stop to place emergency calls
Mobile Facsimile Machine	Wireless document transmission to and from en route trucks	• drivers do not have to find a Federal Express or UPS location to send Bill of Lading and other shipping documentation to Dispatch • enhanced customer service and equipment utilization through improved communications between drivers and Dispatch
	Facsimile receipt confirmation	• automatic receipt confirmation ensures that Dispatch and/or a driver has received the transmission
	Automatic redial will continue to attempt transmission until contact is made	• in the event of an out-of-range call, drivers can continue moving without having to stop and re-attempt retransmissions • Dispatch does not have to re-attempt transmissions when a truck not within a cellular calling area
Alphanumeric Pagers	80-character text message display	• enhanced customer service and equipment utilization through improved communications between drivers and Dispatch • ability to send meaningful text messages to drivers, e.g., directions, names, addresses, phone numbers, etc.
	Worn by the driver (not connected to the truck)	• able to contact a driver when he is away from the truck • the company can send personal *emergency* messages to a driver at anytime — a driver benefit

Financial Benefits

The combined financial benefits provided by implementing the three wireless communications system components are based upon the following factors:

- increased revenue resulting from improved *average monthly revenue load miles per truck* through the ability to easily advise drivers of route changes, load availability, and pickup and delivery changes
- eliminated Federal Express and UPS document shipping costs
- reduced 800# calls to Dispatch; drivers will send daily facsimile status and location reports
- reduced wireless communications costs; alphanumeric paging provides the lowest wireless messaging costs—less than 10 percent of a cellular telephone call

Financial benefits provided to USAL by the proposed wireless communications system are as follows

	Intrastate Truck	Interstate Truck
Increased Revenues		
Estimated monthly increase in average revenue load miles per truck	1,500.00	3,000.00
Average revenue per load mile	$1.40	$1.00
Estimated Monthly Increased Gross Revenue per Truck	**$2,100.00**	**$3,000.00**
Reduced Communications Costs		
Estimated monthly reduction in 800# cost; 25 calls per month per driver at $0.40 per call	$10.00	$10.00
Estimated reduction in Federal Express/UPS costs; $9.00 per shipment	27.00	54.00
Estimated Monthly Cost Savings per Truck	**$37.00**	**$64.00**
Added Communications Costs		
Monthly cost for cellular telephone and facsimile machine; 3-year lease	$61.00	$61.00
Monthly cellular access fees	40.00	40.00

	Intrastate Truck	Interstate Truck
Estimated monthly cellular air time fees; 31 calls per month	31.00	31.00
Monthly alphanumeric pager cost; 3-year lease	15.00	15.00
Monthly alphanumeric pager service	20.00	50.00
Total Monthly Cost per Truck	**$167.00**	**$197.00**
Total Monthly Net Revenue Increase per Truck (before variable expenses)	**$1,970.00**	**$2,867.00**
Additional Monthly Gross Revenue	93	133
Miles needed to break even (Monthly Cost – Monthly Savings ÷ Average Revenue per Load Mile)		

6. Section III: Implementation

Section Purpose

The third recommended strategic proposal section focuses entirely on how the seller plans to implement the proposed product or service. If the previous section presents compelling reasons to purchase the proposed product or service, then this section assures the buyer that the seller has planned for the product implementation or service delivery. By using the proposal to disclose their implementation methods or project management practices, a seller satisfies another of the buyer's critical information requirements and sends a strong message about their ability to deliver on the contract. Without this section, the buyer will have many unanswered questions. An experienced sales professional understands the buyer must have information about the implementation or engagement before being able to make a buy decision.

Standard Methods Customized for the Buyer

This third main proposal section should describe the seller's standard implementation methods or project management practices. It should define the steps, phases, and activities that the seller normally follows when implementing the proposed product or delivering the proposed services. This section also should include estimated project or engagement resource requirements and time frames. It provides an ideal opportunity for the seller to overlay the buyer's unique implementation requirements with their standard business methods. The result is a custom project plan that indicates the seller has thought through the how, who, and when.

Section Titles

Since this section profiles the seller's project or engagement management practices, logical titles would include the seller's name. For example:

- Financial & Banking Systems, Inc. Conversion Management
- BTC Project Management Overview
- Haskell, Slayter, and Cantrell: Engagement Practices

Optionally, the seller can use the title to focus this section on the proposed project or engagement. For example:

- Custom Systems Development Methodology
- Audit Services Transition and Engagement Practices
- Westway Plaza Project: Construction Management

Alternative, generic section titles include:

- Implementation Management
- Project Management
- Engagement Management

Standard Subsections

Like the first two strategic proposal sections that have definite subsection requirements, the third proposal section has three recommended subsections:

- **Methods:** implementation, project, engagement, or management methods (or practices)
- **Team:** implementation, project, engagement, or client service team
- **Schedule:** implementation, project, or engagement schedule

To make a decision, a buyer needs to know *how, with whom,* and *when* the seller will implement or provide the services. For some, writing this section is easy—simply describe the company's standard conversion or project management methods. For example, most CPA firms have clearly defined engagement practices: phases and activities for delivering audit, accounting and/or consulting services. However, for companies that do not follow a standard approach for doing business with customers, this section may present a challenge.

Those sellers who do not have formal business methods or practices may want to develop them because they will:

- clearly differentiate the seller and their proposal from competitors
- assure the buyer that the seller has management capabilities and experience
- provide a consistent approach for doing business

A basic project management book provides an excellent information source.

The following pages briefly discuss content considerations of the three suggested subsections followed by an example third section.

Business Methods or Practices

For long-term and/or complex implementations, the seller needs to assure the buyer that they can manage people, resources, logistics, and activities. This proposal subsection provides a convenient location for presenting the seller's business methods or practices. The proposal might use a table format to efficiently present:

- major activities or phases
- phase deliverables or end-products
- buyer review and approval points within each phase

This subsection should not provide the actual proposed project schedule, rather it only should list the major phases (or activities) of the seller's standard implementation, project, or engagement methods. Another subsection uses the phases activities as a basis for an actual implementation schedule.

The Team

Most buyers like the *team* concept especially when the proposed solution involves a complex or long implementation or results in the delivery of ongoing services. The vision of a team of people organized and working towards one goal sends a strong message. It assures the buyer that the seller knows what resources it takes to deliver on the contract. It also demonstrates the seller's willingness to commit these resources to ensure that the buyer achieves the improvement opportunities within the time frame defined in the proposal.

In many situations, the implementation team may consist of buyer and seller representatives. For example, a software vendor needs buyer representatives to develop conversion specifications and custom processing options to implement its system in the buyer's operation. In these situations this subsection should also include the buyer's team members and their roles and responsibilities. Include the following information for each team member:

- organization
- name
- title
- telephone number (for the seller's team members)
- team role responsibilities

Optionally, the seller should include a biographical résumé of each team member in an appendix.

Team Commitment by Project Phase Subsection

The *Team Commitment by Project Phase* is an optional, hybrid subsection. It combines information from two subsections: *Engagement or Project Management Methods* and *Team*. This subsection presents implementation team member commitment levels by phase or activity. It assures the buyer and seller that everyone understands what it will take to implement the proposed solution. For example, a turnkey systems vendor might develop a table to present team commitment levels by phase. The table on the following page clearly defines project staffing requirements by percent of full-time commitment by phase.

Organization	Name	Project Role	Phase					
			1	2	3	4	5	6
First Bank	John Anderson	Conversion Liaison	50	25	25	50	50	25
	Elaine Ratzak	Application Specialist	35	10	25	40	50	10
	Wendall Larson	Application Specialist	35	10	25	40	50	10
	Connie Long	Customer Service Rep.	35	10	25	40	50	10
FinControl Systems	Leslie Parr	Conversion Team Leader	50	50	50	50	50	20
	Susan Ritten	Bank Liaison Rep/	40	20	40	75	90	20
	Bob Williams	Conversion Specialist	90	90	90	50	50	0
	Terry Savalle	Customer Service Rep	50	50	25	75	90	10
	Randy Wilson	Installation Specialist	50	25	25	75	25	10

Schedule

The *Schedule* subsection should assure the buyer that the seller has planned their unique implementation by including:

- activities and realistic dates for completing the project or engagement
- sufficient information to convince the decision makers that the proposal team has worked through the schedule details

This subsection also may include high-level bar charts or tables that reference an appendix or another section for more detail. The *Schedule* subsection will reference the project phases and activities defined in the previous subsection.

CCM Phase	Feb	Mar	Apr	May	June	July
Conversion Analysis and Planning	■					
Preparation and Equipment Acquisition		■				
System Testing and Validation			■			
Installation and Training				■		
Quality Assurance					■	

See the *Conversion Management Methods* subsection for detailed information about each CMM phase and *Appendix G: Conversion Schedule for Citizens National Bank* for detailed activities and dates.

If the seller does not have a defined implementation or engagement methods, then the *Schedule* subsection can do triple duty: (1) define tasks, (2) assign responsibilities, and (3) establish the schedule. For example, a trust company might use the following table.

Activity	Responsibility	Start Date	Stop Date
Draft Trust Agreement	1st National Bank (FNB)	1-19	1-22
Review Trust Agreement	John & Mary Smith	1-26	1-30
Execute Trust Agreement	John & Mary Smith / FNB	2-03	2-07
Transfer Assets to FNB	FNB	2-10	2-28

Design and Development Checklist

Here are the tasks to complete to design and develop the third section of the strategic proposal, Implementation:

1. **Select an appropriate name for the section.** The title "Implementation" is generic. Identifying the proposed product or service better defines the purpose and content of this main section, e.g., Implementation of PowerBank Cash Management System, Consulting Services Implementation, or Proprietary Training—Courseware Implementation.

2. **Review the recommended subsections to include in this main section.**
   - methods (or practices)
   - team
   - schedule
3. **Decide how to title and what to include in the "Implementation Methods" subsection.** Use formal titles and identifiers if available, e.g., Implementation using Electronic Training Systems' Learning Systems Development Methodology. If the seller follows a formal implementation methodology or business practices, use it. Include main project phases; list activities and deliverables for each phase. If a formal implementation management methodology or business practices description does not exist, create one.
4. **Decide how to title and what to include in the "Implementation Team" subsection.** Most buyers like to see a team approach to implementing a product or service into their business. Identify team members from the buyer and seller organizations. Also define roles and responsibilities for each. If using a phased implementation, include team member commitment level for each phase. Use a product or service identifier or the implementation methodology's name in the subsection title, e.g., PowerBank Implementation Team, Learning Systems Development Methodology Team, etc.
5. **Decide how to title and what to include in the "Implementation Schedule" subsection.** If using a phased implementation approach, develop a table or bar chart of the major phases and their estimated start and stop dates. A bar chart provides an excellent graphical illustration of the proposed implementation. Use a product or service identifier or the name of implementation methodology in the subsection title.

Section III Example

The following Section III example is:

- to Citizens National Bank, an independent bank in a Midwestern state

- from Financial Control Systems (FCS), a Phoenix-based software vendor selling turnkey systems (hardware and software) to small- to medium-sized financial institutions

III. FCS Conversion Management

Conversion Management Methods. FCS will use its *Conversion Management Methods* (CMM) to ensure the transition from BDS, Citizens National Bank's current data processor, goes smoothly. CMM represents FCS's *project management approach* for implementing FCSystem Plus 2000. This phase-limited approach includes the following six phases:

- *Conversion Analysis and Planning*
- *Preparation and Equipment Acquisition*
- *Systems Validation and Testing*
- *Installation and Training*
- *System Conversion*
- *Quality Assurance*

The table on page 69 highlights phase activities and deliverables.

***The FCS Conversion Team Approach—Beginning of a* Partnership.** When Citizens National Bank implements FCSystem Plus 2000, it gains the collective banking, operations, and data processing expertise of the FCS staff. This ongoing relationship represents a *partnership* that begins at conversion time and continues as an ongoing alliance.

To create the long-term *partnership,* FCS uses a team approach for conversion. Select staff from Citizens National Bank and FCS will comprise the *Conversion Team* whose first goal is to convert the bank to FCSystem Plus 2000. Their common goal, along with their plans and activities to accomplish this, fosters the development of an ongoing business relationship between Citizens National Bank and FCS—*the partnership.*

See Appendix G: *Financial Control Systems Staff* for biographical information.

The table on page 70 identifies the team members and their responsibilities.

CMM Phase	Phase Activities	Phase Deliverables
Conversion Analysis and Planning	• form Conversion Team • perform site survey and define custom processing requirements • finalize preliminary equipment requirements and configuration	• Equipment and Site Preparation Requirements • Telephone Line Requirements • Application Conversion Specifications
Preparation and Equipment Acquisition	• FSCS Conversion Team members *beta test* Banker 2000 • customer Conversion Team members validate and approve beta test results	• validated and approved test results
Systems Testing and Validation	• FSCS Conversion Team members *beta test* Banker 2000 • customer Conversion Team members validate and approve beta test results	• validated and approved test results
Installation and Training	• equipment installation and testing • initial customer education (on-site) using conversion test files and on-site equipment	• fully tested equipment, completed initial employee education
System Conversion	• final pre-conversion customer education • *convert and balance;* customer validation and approval • *update and balance;* customer validation and approval • live operation	• balanced and validated conversion • Day 1 update files • fully implemented FSCSystem Plus 2000
Quality Assurance	• on-site FSCS Conversion Liaison monitors post-conversion activities • additional customer education, as needed	• Quality Assurance Checklist

Organization	Team Role	Responsibilities
Citizens National Bank	**Conversion Liaison**	• primary customer contact for FSCS • coordinate on-site conversion activities • coordinate communications with FSCS and current data processor and ATM processor
	Deposit Application Specialist	• define DDA, Savings and CD processing requirements: product specifications, interest calculations, reporting, etc.
	Loans Application Specialist	• define Loan processing requirements: I/L, C/L, and mortgage product specifications, reporting, etc.
	Teller Application Specialist	• define Teller operations and processing requirements: journal and validation printing specifications, security requirements, reporting, forms, etc.
Financial Services Control Systems	**Conversion Leader** Dan Miller *Vice President* (414-404-7810)	• coordinates and manages the entire conversion process • maintains adherence to FSCS' Conversion Management Methods • prepares weekly status report for Bank and FSCS management • resolves conversion issues • ensure conversion is on schedule, in balance, and fully operational in preparation for sign-off
	Bank Liaison Representative **Susan Ritten** *Senior Client Representative* (414-404-7820)	• assembles list of Bank's requirements and option preferences • coordinates Bank's pre-conversion activities • communicate conversion and parameter changes to FSCS technical personnel
	Data Conversion Specialist **Bob Williams** *Senior Conversion Analyst* (414-404-7830)	• collects test data from the existing data processing resource • writes and tests data conversion programs • collects Bank data for live conversion • performs actual data conversion • remains at Bank through the first posting cycles
	Conversion Representative **Terry Savalle** *Sr. Conversion Representative* (414-404-7840)	• approves pre-conversion test of Bank's data • delivers pre-conversion training • ensures Conversion Day and subsequent day balancing • delivers post-conversion training and support

The Citizens National Bank Conversion Schedule. Based upon the analysis of Citizen National Bank's current data processing situation and FCS conversion commitments, project activities could begin in mid-July with full conversion in early October. The following table illustrates the schedule for the conversion phases. See Appendix G for a detailed conversion activities schedule.

Phase / Week	1	2	3	4	5	6	7	8	9	10	11	12
Conversion Analysis and Planning	■											
Preparation and Equipment Acquisition		■										
Systems Testing and Validation				■	■	■	■					
Installation and Training								■	■			
Conversion Friday, October 8, 1999											>	
Quality Assurance (ongoing)											■	■

71

7. Section IV: Seller Profile

Section Purpose

The fourth recommended strategic proposal section provides an opportunity for the seller to profile their uniqueness for the buyer. It serves three primary purposes:

- reduces the buyer's perceived risk about making a change and/or doing business with the seller
- profiles the seller's business, people, and organization
- shows how the seller is uniquely qualified to help the buyer achieve their improvement opportunity by linking the proposed solution and its resulting benefits with the seller's ability to deliver on the contract

Standard Wording, Not Proposal Boilerplate

Of the five recommended proposal sections, this fourth contains the most standard wording. However, it does not mean the section represents *Boilerplate;* rather, it means that its contents will require the fewest changes for use with different accounts. The remainder of this chapter reveals that much of the information contained in this section requires considerable thought and effort to develop. However, once developed, the seller will find that they can easily tailor this section to fit each unique sales situation.

Satisfies the Buyer's Information Needs

The fourth recommended proposal section must assure the buyer that the seller has the capabilities and resources to deliver on the contract—successfully implement the proposed solution. If the seller's solution represents a critical purchase, then the decision makers will perceive two types of risk in making the change:

- the company's business and financial risks associated with making a change
- personal risk resulting from making a poor or wrong decision

Consequently, the buyer's need for seller information varies directly with the perceived risk of the proposed solution.

Many sales-driven proposals, as opposed to customer-driven proposals, do little to minimize the buyer's perceived risks. These proposals often start with a section telling all about the seller. They tout annual revenues, number of offices, years in business, and size of staff. A vendor who begins their proposal with indicative information about their company perhaps sends the wrong message to the buyer—the seller is more important than the buyer. A section devoted to describing the seller does little to help the buyer differentiate or understand the seller when it does not explain how the seller is able to perform on the contract or engagement. Further, it does not describe how the seller will work within the partnership, co-manage the profit improvement project, to implement their proposed products or services.

A strategic proposal differentiates the selling organization and their proposed products or services. It gives the seller an opportunity to describe their business and practices while linking them to their proposed products or services. If the custom benefits developed in the second section gives the buyer the impression they are a *niche market of one* for the seller, then a well-crafted fourth proposal section can make the buyer believe that the seller is only in business to provide them products or service. In other words, this section describes how the seller's business profile results in the unique, tailored products or services that provide very buyer-specific benefits or values for the buyer.

The Level Playing Field Dilemma

Research indicates that a typical buyer has little more than cursory contact with unqualified sellers. A buyer, often through a buying committee, may develop *selection criteria* to evaluate qualified vendors in complex sales situations. The buyer quickly drops those sellers who do not

73

meet their criteria while the remaining ones make the *short list*. When the buyer puts a seller on their *short list,* he arbitrarily places him on a level playing field. In reality, the level playing field can distort the buyer's ability effectively to evaluate the competition because they:

- think all *short list* sellers are equally qualified to deliver on the contract
- begin to focus more on price and availability, rather than value, as the primary differentiator between the competitors

The fourth proposal section cannot help the seller combat the buyer's attempt to differentiate solely on price and availability; however, it can provide an unparalleled opportunity for the seller to rise above the level playing field. A well-crafted fourth section gives the seller an opportunity to differentiate their company, people, and the way they do business. It helps the buyer with their "sorting" process by emphasizing:

- unique seller strengths,
- what is different about the seller, and
- why the seller is uniquely qualified to deliver on the contract.

Section Titles

Since this section profiles the seller, logical titles would include the seller's name. For example:

- Financial & Banking Systems Profile
- XRON: Management Overview
- Haskell, Slayter, and Cantrell: Business Profile

Profile and Practices Subsection Variations

Unlike the first three strategic proposal sections that have definite subsection requirements, the fourth proposal section will vary by the seller's business type. However, at a minimum, most sellers need to include the following four subsections:

- mission statement or customer service philosophy
- company or corporate overview
- quality
- why us?

The buyer's information needs and their perceived risks should strongly influence what a seller might include in this section. Sales professionals who leverage the buyer-seller partnership are able to identify unique subsection requirements and thereby ensure that their proposal meets the buyer's expectations. The seller's business type also helps determine which subsections to use in the third proposal section. For example, a management consultant or consulting services organization might consider the following subsections:

- status meetings and reporting
- engagement or project budget considerations

An equipment manufacturer might use subsections to describe its:

- research and development
- design staff
- production facilities and equipment
- production capacities
- product quality standards

A software vendor might use the following subsections:

- customer service staff and resources
- customer support and training
- software design and development methods
- design and development staff
- facilities and equipment
- product quality
- professional services

Example Subsections

The following pages briefly discuss content considerations of the six suggested subsections followed by an example third section.

Mission or Customer Service Philosophy Statement

One of the best ways to assure the buyer that the seller can deliver on the contract is to include their mission statement or customer service philosophy in the proposal. Often these one or two paragraphs are very customer-centered and clearly define the seller's concerns for product and service quality. For that reason, some sellers prefer to begin the fourth section with their mission statement.

Company or Corporate Overview

This subsection should provide the buyer with indicative seller data such as annual revenues, number of employees, number of locations, etc. Depending on the buyer's needs or selection criteria, the seller may find it advantageous to customize this apparently static information. For example, a prospect may only want to work with a small firm. A large firm might use this subsection to emphasize its local office philosophy and continuity of management to overcome this small firm selection criteria.

Quality

Starting in the 1980s, people became more aware of quality in the goods and services they purchased and how they were treated as customers. Many companies responded with "Total Quality Management" programs and their goods and services vastly improved. Perhaps the publicity surrounding the "Quality Movement" has lessened, but many sales organizations and their customers now have high quality expectations. Therefore, a *Quality* Subsection provides the seller with an ideal location to discuss their product or service quality, ongoing quality programs, and quality awards. Several well-written paragraphs can provide the necessary buyer assurances and meet their expectations. For example,

- service providers might describe their quality customer service commitment
- consulting services firms or consultants might discuss how they ensure quality during the engagement and its relationship to the engagement budget
- manufacturers might describe their quality assurance processes, programs, and standards

Customer References

One of the Section IV subsections should include a list of customer references, or preferably, one subsection should direct the reader to an appendix listing customer references. Buyers need to be assured that the seller can perform on the contract and one of the best ways to provide this assurance is to provide a list of satisfied customers. A later chapter provides content suggestions for a customer reference appendix.

Why Us?

The *Why Us?* subsection is always the last subsection in Section IV. It culminates the creative portion of the proposal, since the fifth and last section deals only with business issues. Ironically, most sellers do not include *Why Us* subsections in their proposals. They miss the opportunity to link three critical components of the sale and proposal. (1) the seller's proposed solution and (2) their value adding benefits and capabilities to deliver on the contract with (3) the buyer's key selection criteria.

Most sellers feel at this point in the sales and proposal process, this critical linkage should be obvious to the decision makers. However, a well-written *Why Us?* subsection makes the linkages for the reader and sends a strong differentiation message about the seller.

Design and Development Checklist

Complete these tasks to design and develop the fourth section of the strategic proposal, Seller Profile:

1. **Select an appropriate name for the section.** The title *Seller Profile* is too generic. A more appropriate section title would include the seller's name, e.g., PowerBank Systems Profile, McFadden & Mayer Profile, etc.
2. **Review and decide which of the four recommended subsections to include in this main section.**

   - mission statement or customer service philosophy
   - company or corporate overview
   - quality
   - why us?

3. **Review the *Profile and Practices Subsection Variations* section** from this chapter to select other subsections to include in this main proposal section.
4. **Design and Development Tip.** Since this section contains more standard wording than any other strategic proposal section, ask the Marketing Department for help in developing each subsection.
5. **Put yourself in the buyer's position to write the *Why Us?* subsection.** Review the buyer's needs and objectives and then identify which product features or service capabilities most strongly support the buyer. Also identify key implementation issues that would make the buyer want to select the proposing company. Finally, identify one or two seller profile components that would support the buyer's selection criteria for choosing the proposing company.

Section IV Example

The following Section IV example follows on with the example from Section III:

- to Citizens National Bank, an independent bank in a Midwestern state
- from Financial Control Systems (FCS), a Phoenix-based software

78

vendor selling turnkey systems (hardware and software) to small- to medium-sized financial institutions

IV. FCS Profile

FCS Mission Statement. *Financial Control Systems is the premier provider of data processing systems to the financial services industry. FCS operates with the highest degree of integrity, provides quality products and service, and maintains a steadfast commitment to excellence.*

Corporate History

7/95	Financial Control Systems (FCS) founded
10/96	IBM announces FCS as a *National Business Partner*
2/97	FCS introduces the *FCSystem 2000* family of software at the ABA National Operations & Automation Conference
5/97	FCS successfully installs the first *FCSystem 2000* beta site
2/98	SCO, a leading UNIX software vendor, invites FCS to become a *National Development Partner*
3/98	FCS introduces the *FCSystem Plus 2000* product line to the banking community
7/98	FCS acquires Pegasus, Inc., a Denver-based platform automation company with over 200 clients
10/99	FCS acquires PCATM, Inc., a Milwaukee-based ATM software company with 25 worldwide clients
11/99	FCS installs *FCSystem Plus 2000* at the 20th customer site

Customer Service: Philosophy and Practices. The FCS Mission Statement clearly reflects the company's customer service philosophy:

> *FCS operates with integrity, provides quality products and service, and maintains a steadfast commitment to excellence.*

At FCS, this philosophy goes beyond words. FCS has a unique *employee incentive program* that rewards its customer service and technical staff for maintaining high levels of customer service excellence. The FCS Customer Service Center operates under extended service hours: 7:00 A.M. to 7:00 P.M. CST, Monday through Friday and 7:00 A.M. to 3:00 P.M. CST on Saturday.

Customer Service staff complete a rigorous six-month training program that includes two months of on-site experience at a local FCS cus-

79

tomer location and two months with an FCS Conversion Team. All staff members must have an undergraduate degree. Most have degrees in accounting, business administration, or computer science.

FCS Quality Commitment. FCS maintains a *steadfast commitment to excellence* as stated in its mission statement . . . *FCS operates with the highest degree of integrity, provides quality products and service* . . . For a bank data processing organization, quality must be present in four areas: software, hardware, customer service, and people. As you have read to this point, FCS certainly plays close attention to the first two areas. However, for a bank to effectively measure all four areas requires time and experience. We invite you to contact our existing customers, *our partners,* to gauge our quality commitment. See Appendix H: *FCS Customer References* for more information.

Why FCS? Citizens National Bank has defined several strategic objectives for which FCS and FCSystem Plus 2000 provides cost effective and comprehensive solutions. Specifically:

- automate all departments as a means to increase overall employee productivity
- reduce and control data processing costs
- grow the organization at low incremental operational costs
- gain marketing advantages over the competition
- move to in-house systems that employ *Open Systems Architecture*

FCSystem Plus 2000 using *Open Systems Architecture* offers the best option for Citizens National Bank to:

- select and integrate the best applications for its current and future data processing needs
- use off-the-shelf, low-cost hardware alternatives
- increase its employees productivity through the user- friendly and user-familiar operations of *Open Systems*

Through its *Conversion Management Methods* and *Conversion Team* approach, FCS can ensure a smooth transition from the bank's current data processing systems.

8. Section V: Business Issues

Section Purpose

The fifth and last main proposal section, *Business Issues,* serves only one purpose, to present the business side of the proposed solution. It should answer any questions the buyer may have about:

- the seller's basic assumptions for estimating implementation timing and calculating prices
- what are the fees and/or prices and what additional expenses the buyer will incur for the seller to implement products or services or to complete the engagement
- when and for how much will the seller invoice the buyer

One of this section's primary goals is to avoid buyer surprises after the sale. Therefore, the seller can clearly document all the business issues regarding the proposed solution.

Section Titles

Some alternative section titles might include the seller's name or the name of the proposed product or service:

- Haskell and Smith: Engagement Issues
- ProSchedule Plus: Business Concerns
- TowRight Trailers: Business Issues

Alternate generic section titles include the following:

- Business Plans
- Business Considerations
- Commitments and Costs

Recommended Subsections

Most sellers will find that three subsections suffice in the last strategic proposal section:

- *Assumptions*
- *Fees/Prices and Other Expenses*
- *Invoicing Schedule*

Assumptions Subsection

The following definition points out why and how a seller's assumptions often create problems after the sale.

as·sump·tion *n.* **1.** The act of taking for granted. **2.** Something taken for granted or accepted as true without proof; a supposition. **3.** Presumption; arrogance. **4.** *Logic.* A minor premise.

Typically, the seller must make assumptions about certain aspects of the buyer's business, operations, and staff to establish fees/prices, assign staff, and schedule an implementation. Sellers usually base their assumptions on:

- pertinent aspects of the buyer's business and operations
- past experiences with similar engagements, projects, implementations, or production scenarios
- estimates of the scope and magnitude of the proposed solution
- estimates of business and economic trends

A well-written *Assumptions* subsection should answer any remaining questions the buyer may have about the proposed product or service that were not answered in the previous proposal sections. Buyers respect the seller's openness because it demonstrates the mutual trust and confidence of the buyer-seller partnership.

Sellers should follow two rules when developing assumptions for their strategic proposals:

Rule #1: Include only critical assumptions.

Rule #2: Rewrite the proposed solution and/or implementation sections if too many assumptions are needed.

The proposal should not include obvious or nonessential assumptions. It should list only critical assumptions used to develop the proposed solution. Some examples of critical assumptions:

- To adhere to the implementation schedule, a software development consultant might assume the buyer will review and approve design documents within five business days of receipt.
- To maintain the listed equipment prices, a manufacturer might assume certain raw material costs will not increase by more than 10 percent over current costs during scheduled production.
- To receive the quoted audit fee, the CPA firm might assume that the client will provide specific types and levels of administrative support.

When a proposal contains too many critical assumptions, it usually signals a problem with an inadequately defined proposed solution or implementation section. If most of the assumptions relate to the proposed solution, the proposal team needs to convert some of the assumptions into product or service specifications. Some examples:

- A software vendor's proposal lists an assumption that the buyer will have IBM's OS/2 operating system installed on their personal computers. The OS/2 operating system is actually a software product specification, not an assumption about the buyer's computer system configuration.
- A machinery manufacturer's proposal might include an assumption that states the buyer will have 220V electrical service at the installation site. The 220V electrical service is an operating specification for the machine, not an assumption about the customer's facilities.

If most of the assumptions relate to implementation issues, the proposal team needs to review the level of detail and content of the implementation methodology, team, and schedule subsections. Perhaps they need to convert some of the assumptions into implementation parameters.

Fees or Prices (and Other Expenses) Subsection

By the time the proposal recipient reaches the *Fees/Prices* subsection, he or she will have seen the seller's fee or price two times, once in the *Executive Summary* and again in the *Financial Benefits* subsection of *Section II: Proposed Solution*. However, the fees/prices listed in those two locations typically provide only a summarized total. The *Fees/Prices* subsection provides the seller with an opportunity to present detailed calculations and explanations. Remember, the goal of this entire section is to avoid buyer surprises. This subsection needs to disclose and detail total buyer costs.

The contents of this subsection will vary from seller to seller depending on the:

- seller's business type or profession and accepted fee or pricing practices
- buyer's fees/prices information needs and expectations
- need to disclose fees or prices by project phase to support progress payment invoices
- need to list quantity, description, unit price, and extended price for products or product components
- need to define project-related expenses, e.g., freight, travel costs, duplication, etc.

Some examples:

- A management consultant might list her hourly rate, estimated hours for the engagement, and total estimated engagement fee. Additionally, the consultant should include estimated travel expenses, if any, in the proposal.
- A professional services firm might list fees by project phase with a grand total for the project. Additionally, the proposal should include estimated travel expenses, if any.
- A manufacturer might list quantities, descriptions, unit prices, and extended prices for the proposed equipment components. Additionally, the proposal should include applicable taxes and freight.

Invoicing Schedule Subsection

A strategic proposal defines how and when the seller will invoice the buyer for the proposed product or service. The seller should avoid surprising the buyer with unexpected invoices for such things as initial materials procurement or monthly travel expenses. The *Invoicing Schedule* subsection becomes most important when the timing of an invoice is tied to the completion of a major project phase or deliverable or invoicing is non-routine. For example, a computer systems integrator may invoice the buyer for:

- hardware costs upon acceptance of the proposal or signing of the contract
- software costs at the end of an installation phase
- travel expenses at the end of each month

Further, to work within the buyer's budget, the seller may agree not to send an invoice until budgeted funds become available. This may happen at the end of the buyer's fiscal year. In these situations, the buyer can make a commitment and the seller can begin production or implementation activities with the understanding that no invoices will be sent before an agreed to date.

Design and Development Checklist

Complete these tasks to design and develop the fifth section of the strategic proposal, Seller Profile:

1. **Select an appropriate name for the section.** The title *Business Issues* may be too generic or may not be appropriate for the target buyers. An optional section title might be Costs and Commitments or might include the proposed product or service name, e.g., Business Issues: PowerBank Systems, Single Source Graphics Program Costs and Commitments, etc.
2. **Review and decide which of the three recommended subsections to include in this main section.**
   - assumptions
   - fees/prices

85

- invoicing schedule

3. **Decide how to title and what to include in the "Assumptions" subsection.** Use titles and identifiers to focus the content, e.g., TOTAL Systems Implementation Assumptions or Project Management Assumptions. For readability, use numbers or bullets to list critical assumptions used to develop the proposed solution.

4. **Decide how to title and what to include in the "Fees/Prices" subsection.** Use titles and identifiers to make this subsection title less generic, e.g., Audit and Tax Service Fees, ProServe Licensing and Maintenance Fees, etc. Make sure the financial details contained in this subsection reflect the summarized fee and price information contained elsewhere in the Proposal: Executive Summary and Section II: Proposed Solution. Remember, write this subsection to avoid buyer surprises after the contract is signed—include all costs that the buyer will incur.

5. **Decide how to title and what to include in the "Invoicing Schedule" subsection.** Use a less generic subsection title to link with the proposed product or service, e.g., Consulting Services Engagement: Invoicing Schedule, Licensing and Maintenance Fee Invoicing Schedule, etc. List all scheduled payments including when and how much. Also include any appropriate terms and conditions.

Section V Example

The following Section IV example is:

- to SC Trucking, a medium-size, trucking company located in Dallas, Texas
- from Advanced Wireless Concepts Systems, Inc. (AWS), a company specializing in wireless communications systems integration applications

V. Commitments and Costs

Assumptions. WCS made the following assumptions when pricing the proposed services and equipment:

- SC Trucking (SCT) will lease all equipment.
- AWC will install the cellular telephones and mobile facsimile machines at SCT facilities in Dallas, Texas.

Implementation Costs. AWC will install the communications equipment in SCT trucks over a five (5) month period. The estimated schedule is as follows:

Month	# of Installations	Monthly Implementation Costs
June	30	$11,250
July	45	$17,280
August	60	$23,040
September	75	$28,800
October	75	$28,800

The above table lists monthly implementation costs. Per truck costs to begin service are:

Equipment Lease Deposit	$161.00
Advance Lease Payments (3 months)	$183.00
Connect Fee (one-time)	$ 40.00
	$384.00

Monthly Fees. Monthly fees for the cellular phones and mobile facsimile machines are as follows:

	Intrastate Truck	Interstate Truck
monthly cost for Mobile Fax Machine (3-year lease)	$61.00	$61.00
monthly cellular service fees:		
access fee	$40.00	$60.00
estimated air time: 31 calls/month	$31.00	$31.00
Total Monthly Cost/Truck	**$132.00**	**$152.00**

Invoicing Schedule. AWC will invoice SC Trucking as follows:

- **Implementation Costs** are invoiced at the end of each month for installations completed during the month.
- **Monthly Cellular Service Fees** are invoiced the first week of each month based on the previous month's actual air times, including transmission detail by telephone number (truck).

9. Important Proposal Components

In addition to the five main proposal sections, a strategic proposal has other quality components that can help differentiate it from the competition: the *Executive Summary,* the *Transmittal Letter,* the *Title Page, Table of Contents,* and *Appendices.* This chapter will discuss design and development issues for each component and presents examples.

Positioning the Reader

Some decision makers have such busy schedules that it is impossible for them to read an entire proposal; they may only "flip" through it. While flipping, the proposal's structure, layout, and overall appearance may subtly communicate quality. However, most will not make a critical buying decision with just a cursory review of the proposal. Some decision makers may take the easiest path and wait until the seller's presentation to learn about the improvement opportunity and the proposed solution. Other decision makers may only read the Executive Summary and perhaps the Transmittal Letter. They know from experience that these two proposal elements, if well-crafted, will provide them with a synopsis of the document and valuable insight into the sales situation. They may rely entirely on these two proposal components to prepare for the seller's upcoming sales presentation. In these situations, the Transmittal Letter and Executive Summary play a critical role in positioning the reader and the key account sale.

In other instances, the Transmittal Letter and Executive Summary may serve to convince the decision maker that the proposed solution is viable and needs further consideration. After flipping through a proposal and reading the Executive Summary and/or Transmittal Letter, some decision makers may think the proposal's improvement opportunity and proposed solution have merit. They may then pass the proposal on to a subordinate for a second opinion. Of course, most subordinates cannot flip through t' proposal; they are obligated to read the entire document and report ba' their managers.

By design, a well-written Transmittal Letter and Executive ᶜ presents the seller with an opportunity to position those recipients who want to or must read the entire proposal. The Transmittal Letter positions readers because it presents the reasons that the seller is presenting the proposal and highlights critical issues concerning the buyer's improvement opportunity and seller's proposed solution.

The Executive Summary positions readers because it captures the proposal's essence by providing summary information on all the key points it contains. It symbolically sets critical information alert flags throughout the proposal's main sections.

Transmittal Letter

A sales professional will include a Transmittal Letter when sending or delivering the proposal because it represents good business etiquette. It is the proposal's cover letter and is addressed to the *Internal Sponsor* or whomever requested the proposal. Optionally, the seller may bind a copy of the Transmittal Letter in every proposal so that all recipients have an opportunity to read it. The Transmittal Letter should be no more than two pages long. It should:

- relate why the seller is submitting the proposal, e.g., at the request of the buyer or in response to a Request for Proposal
- highlight the buyer's improvement opportunity and how implementing the proposed solution ensures that the buyer reduces costs, increases profits, or improves operations
- include a summary of the seller's *Why Us?* subsection
- include the sales professional's offer to provide additional information or assistance if requested by the buyer
- thank the buyer and his or her staff for their time and efforts in developing the proposal

The sales professional should use company stationery for the Transmittal Letter.

Transmittal Letter Example

First American Bank
1 Main Street
Denver, CO 80010

May 19, 1998

Ms. Wendy P. Willowsby
11 Lombardy Court
Denver, Colorado 87528

Dear Ms. Willowsby:

After a careful review of your unique situation and needs and at your request, I am submitting the enclosed proposal for your consideration. In our last meeting, we concluded that a *Revocable Grantor Trust* with First American Bank (FAB) serving as Trustee will provide an excellent vehicle for managing your investments by:

- helping you achieve your two primary investment goals: (1) provide for your two nephews' college education and (2) meet your defined early retirement income levels
- offering full-time investment control and management

As your Trustee, FAB enters into a *fiduciary relationship* with you. By definition, a *fiduciary relationship* is dedicated to providing personalized trust and investment services as opposed to investment management agreements that are designed to aid the sale of transaction and commission-based products. Further, FAB represents a legal entity whose existence will ensure continuity of service even though its officers and staff may change.

The enclosed proposal includes a detailed description of a *Revocable Grantor Trust* with FAB. It defines nonfinancial and financial benefits specific to your personal situation and investment portfolio. Please call me if you have questions or want to discuss any aspect of the proposal.

Thank you again for considering First American Bank for this important decision. I have thoroughly enjoyed our meetings and look forward to becoming a member of your *Trust Relationship Team.*

Sincerely,

Lee H. Trenton
First Vice President and Trust Officer

LHT/ms

Executive Summary

The Executive Summary is the first component of the strategic proposal. Some trace its origins back to the voluminous proposals prepared for the federal government by defense and other contractors. The sheer size of their proposals forced these contractors to summarize proposal content so that a reader could get a high-level overview of the proposed sale before trying to read the complete document. The Executive Summary was absolutely essential for properly positioning the proposal's recipients.

A few salespeople think writing an Executive Summary is a mistake because it gives the recipient an opportunity to avoid reading the entire proposal. In reality, the Executive Summary serves a critical purpose and is more needed than ever in today's fast-paced environment. Ironically, many decision makers will read only the Executive Summary. They expect and need a concise synopsis of the improvement opportunity and the proposed solution. This fact may make the Executive Summary the single-most important proposal component. It must represent the seller's best writing skills. In reality, the Executive Summary represents a *proposal in miniature* because it captures the most important aspects of each of the four main proposal sections and contains all the information needed to make a buying decision.

Executive Summary Writing Tips

The proposal team should use the following tips when writing an Executive Summary:

Write it last. The Executive Summary represents a condensed version of the proposal. It should not be written until the proposal is finished.

Make it a miniature proposal. If some decision makers read only the Executive Summary, then it must capture the key points of the entire proposal.

Follow these steps when writing the Executive Summary:

1. Using the final proposal draft, identify the most critical information from each section.
2. With the critical information as a guide, condense each section into one or two paragraphs.
3. Combine the paragraphs into the Executive Summary.
4. Optionally, use the proposal's main section titles to create subsections in the Executive Summary.

Control its length. The "perfect" Executive Summary would require only one page; however, this is an imperfect world and some Executive Summaries may be two, three, or more pages. Further, the proposal's page format and layout can affect length. It is better to have two or three pages of easy-to-read, nicely formatted text than one full page of text using a 10-point font. As a rule of thumb, an Executive Summary should not exceed four or five pages even for a hundred-plus page proposal.

Executive Summary Example

The following pages contain an example Executive Summary.

Background Information. Granger Motor Freight (GMF) provides interstate freight service between the mid-Atlantic coast and California. With 600+ employees, GMF operates 200 trucks that generated $44.9 million in revenues in 1998. Most of GMF's customers are small- to medium-sized businesses located within 100 miles of main east-west interstate highways. These customers normally do not ship full loads. Consequently, GMF is able to combine several partial loads and charge premium prices.

Once a GMF truck leaves one of the eleven GMF facilities, communications between dispatch and drivers is totally dependent on land-line telephone communications. GMF requires its drivers to call dispatch once a day using an 800 number. Dispatch can contact en route trucks only if they are able to reach drivers at a scheduled customer pickup or delivery point or at another GMF facility. A survey conducted by GMF and ProCell Corporation (PCC) staff found that GMF's sole dependence on land-line communications between truck dispatch personnel and en route drivers is resulting in lost revenues and inefficient routing. GMF's average truck load capacity is 83 percent, which indicates excess capacity; however, some customers have to wait up to three or four days for freight pickups because dispatch is unable to easily communicate with en route trucks.

Proposed Cellular Solution. After reviewing current operations and business communications needs, PCC proposes GMF install cellular telephones in its 200 trucks. Providing cellular telephone communications capabilities between truck dispatch personnel and en route trucks will provide operational, employee, and customer service benefits for GMF:

- ability to quickly and easily make schedule and route changes—better customer service
- immediate access to en route drivers in case of a family emergency
- direct access to repair personnel and facilities for drivers in case of an on-road breakdown
- ability to notify dispatch of travel delays and equipment breakdowns

The ability to change the schedules and routes of en route trucks using cellular telephone communications will provide the following estimated financial benefits:

• Reduced annual operating costs:	$ 192,000
• Increased annual freight revenues:	1,122,000
Total	**$ 1,314,000**

The total cellular telephone equipment costs for 200 GMF trucks is **$64,900.** Estimated annual costs are:

• Cellular service fees based on a two-year agreement):	$920,000
• Equipment depreciation (three-year basis):	40,000
Total Cost	**$960,000**

- This results in annual increases in pre-tax profits over the two- year agreement period: **$354,000**
- The estimated return on investment (ROI): **545%**

94

ProCell Corporation Practices. Upon acceptance of this proposal, GMF staff and the PCC Account Team will form a *Cellular Service Partnership.* This partnership will direct equipment installation and employee education activities. Within one month PCC will install and activate all cellular telephones.

ProCell Corporation Profile. ProCommunications Corporation, the parent company of PCC, is one of the world's leading telecommunications companies. PCC is the tenth largest U.S. cellular company, with over 5,000 employees. It has been at the forefront of cellular communications since the industry's birth in 1983. PCC's 1998 revenues were $1.4 billion.

PCC is not just another cellular service provider. It is *Your national cellular resource.* PCC's reputation and future relies on its ability to consistently provide the best and most advanced cellular technology. When GMF selects PCC as its cellular service, it begins a *Cellular Service Partnership.* GMF gains the expertise and services of its PCC Account Team, a group of professionals who can access other PCC resources to:

- provide GMF employee education
- develop and refine unique wireless communications strategies
- ensure that GMF has access to the latest and most innovative cellular services and equipment

No other company matches PCC depth of knowledge and commitment to service.

Business Issues. PCC will require GMF to provide a purchase order(s) covering purchase for the cellular equipment ($64,900) and two-year service agreements.

Other Design and Development Issues

In addition to the five main proposal sections, the Executive Summary, and the Transmittal Letter, a strategic proposal has other quality components that can help differentiate it from the competition, the *Title Page, Table of Contents,* and *Appendices.*

95

Title Page

Like a book, a strategic proposal needs a title page. It should include the:

- proposal's title
- recipient's name
- the seller's name
- submission date

This page also provides a good place for the seller's logo. Optionally, the seller also may include the buyer's logo. However, some organizations do not want anyone reproducing their logos; therefore, the seller should obtain permission from the buyer before using their logo.

Title

The proposal team has some options to consider before selecting the title; it can either:

- describe the proposed improvement opportunity and emphasize its benefits and results, or
- simply list the name of the proposed product or service

The buyer-seller partnership should select a title that they feel is most appropriate for the buying organization and its decision makers. For example, an employee personality testing company could title a proposal with either of the following titles:

- *Reducing Employee Turnover through Personality Profile Testing* or
- *ProSelect Personality Profile Testing*

Both titles are appropriate, although the first title is more effective because it includes an important benefit the buyer will realize and also identifies the proposed solution.

Recipient's and Seller's Names. Use the buying and selling organizations' full names. For individuals, use first names, middle initials, and last names. Do not use nicknames, abbreviations, or acronyms. For example:

Correct	Incorrect
Multimedia Learning Systems, Inc.	MLS
Idaho Commerce Bank, N.A.	ICB
McGregor & Paulson, LLP	M&P
John A. Smith & Mary L. Smith	Mr. & Mrs. John Smith
James R. Thorton, III	Jim Thorton

The title page should link the buyer's and seller's names, thereby establishing the improvement opportunity (buyer-seller) partnership for the decision makers. Some examples:

- A Personal Trust Services Proposal to Lawrence J. Finley, Jr. from Wisconsin Commerce Bank
- A Thompson Consulting Group Solution for Acme Manufacturing Company

Submission Date. Use the date that the proposal will be formally presented to the buyer. Note: the date on the title page and that of the *Transmittal Letter* should match. Write out the date: month, day, and year; do not use a numerical date. For example, October 17, 1998 versus 10/17/98 or 10-17-98.

Title Page Example. The following pages contain title page examples.

Title Page: Example 1

FCSystem Plus 2000

A Data Processing Proposal to

Citizens National Bank

from

Financial Control Systems

September 15, 1998

Title Page: Example 2

Controlling Workplace Substance Abuse

A National Institute on Drug Prevention

Solution

for

Pacific Food Systems, Inc.

May 29, 1998

Table of Contents

The Table of Contents provides a road map for the reader. It serves two purposes: (1) provides a structural view of the proposal and (2) helps the reader locate specific information. It should include the titles or names and page numbers of:

- sections
- subsections
- appendices

Page Numbering

Follow these simple rules to number proposal pages:

- Number all pages except the Title Page
- The Table of Contents and the Executive Summary should use lower case Roman numerals as page numbers, e.g., the first page of the Table of Contents is page "i."
- Number pages in the five main sections consecutively; the first page of the first proposal section is page "1."
- Use each appendix's alphabetic designation as part of the page number, e.g., the third page of Appendix C would be C-3.

Table of Contents Example. The next page contains a sample Table of Contents.

Table of Contents
Executive Summary	i
Section I: Background Information	
A. PagePro Company Background	1
B. Current Transmission Configuration	1
C. PagePro New Business Opportunities	2
D. PagePro Needs and Objectives	2
E. Purpose of This Proposal	2
Section II: Proposed ProCheck+	
A. Product Description	3
B. PagePro Business Application	3
C. Nonfinancial Benefits	4
D. Financial Benefits	4

Section III: TellPage Strategic Partnership
   A. TellPage Partnership Practices   5
   B. Partnership Team   6
   C. Project Schedule   7
Section IV: TellPage Profile and Technology
   A. TellPage Profile   8
   B. Patented TellPage Technology   8
   C. Research & Development   9
   D. Customer and Technical Service   9
   E. Wireless Communications Quality   10
   F. Why TellPage?   10
Section V: Business Issues
   A. Assumptions   11
   B. Revenue Sharing   11
   C. Other Financial Issues   12
Appendices
   A. Wireless Information Market Analysis   A-1
   B. ProCheck+ Revenue Analysis: PagePro   B-1
   C. TellPage: Leading Edge Wireless Information   C-1

Appendices

Proposal appendices serve two primary purposes. They:

- help the writer maintain the proposal's flow of information and ideas by providing a means to control length and detail level
- provide a place to locate, organize, and label preprinted materials, e.g., brochures, specifications, cost analyses, etc.

Maintain the Flow

A well-written proposal will hold its readers' attention with its logical flow of information and ideas. Although it's essential to provide sufficient detail to support key points within the proposal, the proposal should never overload readers with excessive or irrelevant information. Too much detail may confuse readers, or worse, it may cause some readers to miss the critical reasons why the buyer needs to make a change.

For example, a software vendor used an implementation checklist when converting new clients to their system. The checklist contained 167 activities or items and the vendor included it in their proposals to demonstrate their experience. The checklist contained essential information and assured the buyer that the seller knew how to handle conversions; however, putting it in a main proposal section overwhelmed all but the most technical readers. To remedy this information overload situation, the software vendor:

- developed a standard conversion method using six major phases
- assigned each of the 167 activities to one of the six conversion phases
- listed the six phases, including their estimated start and stop dates, in the proposal and referenced the appendix that listed the 167 activities with their estimated start and stop dates

Preprinted Materials

The overall appearance of a proposal is ruined when the seller includes preprinted materials in main proposal sections. Preprinted materials will interrupt a proposal's flow of information and ideas. Often when a writer puts a brochure or specifications sheet in the middle of a proposal section, he or she wants the recipient to find critical information in the document. The recipient would be better served if the seller summarized the information in one or two paragraphs and used the preprinted material as a supporting appendix.

For example, a computer hardware vendor, who builds automated cassette tape systems for data storage, should not put the technical specifications for their new system in *Section II: Proposed Solutions.* Rather, the proposal writer should: (1) briefly describe the new system (2) explain how it will work in the buyer's environment, and (3) put the system's technical specifications in an appendix. Remember the business versus technical proposal discussion in an early chapter. Most decision makers have little interest in the technical specifications; they assume the proposed product or service will work as described. Their main interest lies in the benefits provided by the seller's proposed solution.

Two Rules

Two rules guide the use of appendices:

1. **Rule #1: Avoid dangling appendices.** Do not include an appendix that is not referenced in at least one main proposal section.
2. **Rule #2: Follow order of reference.** The sequence of appendices should follow the order in which they are referenced in the main proposal, e.g., the first referenced appendix is A, the next one referenced is B, etc.

Common Appendices and Guidelines. The table below identifies common proposal appendices and provides some guidelines for their use.

Appendix	Use Guidelines / Comments
Cost Analysis	• highlight critical assumptions and numbers in the proposal; put spreadsheet reports in an appendix
Biographical Resumes	• only list staff names and titles in the proposal • optionally, include a one or two sentence summary of critical skills or accomplishments • follow a standard format for biographical resumes
Implementation or Project Methods	• include major phases or tasks and deliverables in the proposal; use the appendix to list detail methods activities
Installation Schedule	• list the main phases or tasks with their start and stop dates or as a bar chart (with dates) in the proposal; use an appendix for schedule detail or a detailed bar chart
Client References	• do not list client names in the proposal, or only list a few well-known names; rather, reference the appendix containing the client list • client references should include the following information: company name and address, contact name, title, and telephone number, and a brief project or engagement overview • ensure that the client approves of the reference and that all client information is current

How to Use an Appendix. This example shows how a proposal writer can condense the following lengthy table contained in an appendix to a smaller table or one sentence to control the length and detail level of a proposal section.

Appendix E

Acme Manufacturing: CAI Test Project

Phase	Name/Activities	Start	Stop
1	**Analysis & Design**	04-20-96	05-13-96
2	**Detail Design**	05-20-96	06-12-96
	· Selection Tests	05-20-96	06-12-96
	· CAI Design	05-20-96	06-12-96
3	**Development**	06-11-96	07-23-96
	· Selection Tests	06-11-96	07-02-96
	· CAI	06-15-96	07-23-96
4	**Testing**	07-16-96	08-05-96
	· Selection Tests	07-16-96	07-22-96
	· CAI	07-16-96	08-05-96
5	**Implementation**	07-09-96	08-26-96
	· AESS (software)	07-09-96	07-21-96
	· Tests	07-29-96	08-26-96
	· CAI	08-10-96	08-26-96
6	**Operation**	09-03-96	ongoing

The writer could develop a smaller table for the main proposal and include only the main phases.

PHASE	NAME/ACTIVITIES	START	STOP
1	**Analysis & Design**	04-20-96	05-13-96
2	**Detail Design**	05-20-96	06-12-96
3	**Development**	06-11-96	07-23-96
4	**Testing**	07-16-96	08-05-96
5	**Implementation**	07-09-96	08-26-96
6	**Operation**	09-03-96	ongoing

See Appendix E, *Acme Manufacturing: CAI Test Project* for schedule details.

Or the writer could condense the information into two sentences. The CAI Test Project will start in late April and is scheduled to be operational in early September. See Appendix E, *Acme Manufacturing: CAI Test Project* for schedule details.

10. The Strategic Letter Proposal

Design Perspective

When many people think of a sales proposal, they can visualize only a monstrous three-ring binder filled with pages and pages of information, specifications, tables, and other marketing materials. Some think all proposals have to be long to be good, while others equate length or size with importance—the longer or larger the proposal the greater its importance. Certainly, some sellers must write 15–30 page proposals because of the complexity of their products or services or because of the complexity of their application. However, some sellers will find that many of their proposals will require only five to ten pages and are most effective in a letter format, the *letter proposal.*

As its name implies, the strategic *letter proposal* incorporates all the logic and content requirements of normal strategic proposal, but, in a smaller package. Visualize a letter proposal fitting between an Executive Summary and a standard strategic proposal. On one end, the Executive Summary is a proposal in miniature; in one to four pages, it provides the reader with a synopsis of the entire proposal. On the other end, the standard strategic proposal contains all the recommended components: a Transmittal Letter, an Executive Summary, the five recommended main sections, and supporting appendices. The letter proposal is a hybrid. It is longer than an Executive Summary and shorter than a standard strategic proposal. It uses the content structure and information flow specified by the five recommended sections of a strategic proposal but is typically no longer than ten pages. Optionally, a letter proposal also may include appendices or attachments to control its length.

Usage Guidelines

Sales professionals should consider a letter proposal simply another form of a standard strategic proposal. They should use it in the same manner as they use a regular proposal in their integrated sales and proposal development processes. Letter proposals work well when the sales situation matches one or more of the following parameters:

- smaller, less complex and/or lower dollar value sales
- add-on or interim sales after the acceptance of a strategic proposal and completion of a large strategic sale
- sales in which one or two individuals have authority to approve the purchase

Example Situation

For example, *BDS,* a bank data processing systems vendor, closed a major contract with Commercial State Bank six months ago. This contract involved converting the bank's primary data processing functions from a service bureau to BDS's NewBanker 2001, an in-house, turnkey system ($525,000 contract). The major proposal did not include conversion of the bank's teller systems. However, after the bank was converted to New-Banker 2001, the BDS sales professional developed a letter proposal that addressed converting the bank to BDS's NewBanker 2001 Teller hardware and software. The value of the letter proposal was $63,900. In this situation the letter proposal was an appropriate vehicle for communicating the bank's improvement opportunity because: (1) the initial strategic proposal was accepted by the bank less than a year ago and (2) NewBanker 2001 Teller is an integrated NewBanker 2001 component and a very logical add-on sale.

Because of the dollar value of teller system, Commercial State Bank did not need or want a standard strategic proposal from BDS. However, they did want BDS to identify specific nonfinancial and financial benefits and define their implementation plan. The letter proposal provided BDS with an expedient and effective vehicle for this add-on sales situation.

Ideal for Consultants

Many consulting firms and independent consultants find the letter proposal format works extremely well for most of their engagements. It contains all the elements of a standard strategic proposal only in condensed format. It allows the consultant to educate the proposal recipients on all aspects of the improvement opportunity and the benefits of the proposed consulting engagement. Further, the letter format appears less imposing than a standard proposal, even though its message can be just as compelling. Optionally, the letter proposal can contain an *Acceptance* section, with signature lines for the customer to approve the engagement. However, some consultants prefer to attach a standard consulting services agreement to their letter proposals.

For example, Presentation Dynamics, Inc. provides sales presentation design, development, and training services. Most of their consulting engagements range from $8,000 to $20,000. Because of the nature and size of their professional services, they use letter proposals for most engagements. However, for large contracts, such as a multiple office training program for a Fortune 500 client, Presentation Dynamics uses a standard strategic proposal format.

Content and Format

A letter proposal is a strategic proposal in letter format. The first several paragraphs of a letter proposal contain the information normally found in a strategic proposal's Transmittal Letter. Because of its brevity, a letter proposal does not need a Table of Contents or an Executive Summary. Optionally, it can include a section for buyer approval in lieu of a contract or purchase order.

Letter proposals should contain the following components and sections:

Transmittal Letter. The seller should use one or more paragraphs to present some sales situation background.

Strategic Proposal Sections. The standard five strategic proposal sections condensed one or two pages for each section. See Chapters 4 through 8 for detailed information about each of the recommended sections.

Acceptance. This is an optional section containing a signature and date line for an authorized buyer representative to indicate his or her approval to proceed to implementation.

Appendices (or Attachments). Controlling the letter proposal's length is critical; maximum length should be ten pages. Therefore, the seller should use appendices for detailed information. See Chapter 9, *Important Proposal Components* for guidelines on using appendices.

Proposal Section or Component	Standard Proposal	Letter Proposal
Transmittal Letter	yes	yes
Table of Contents	yes	no
Executive Summary	yes	no
Section I: Background Information	yes	yes
Section II: Proposed Business Solution	yes	yes
Section III: Implementation	yes	yes
Section IV: Seller Profile	yes	yes
Section V: Business Issues	yes	yes
Approval (section)	no	yes*
Appendices (or Attachments)	yes	yes*

Letter Proposal Example

Daniels & Associates, Inc.
3412 West Sentinel Drive, Suite 100
Dallas, Texas 75242-7975

October 17, 1999

Mr. Richard P. Kennedy
Vice President, Sales and Marketing
Professional Technologies, Inc.
175 West Conroe Avenue
New London, CT 11111

Dear Mr. Kennedy:

As we discussed, designing and developing practice area sales proposal models for Professional Technologies, Inc. (PTI) presents an opportunity to enhance the company's overall sales process. Organizations that integrate a strategic sales proposal model and supporting tools into their sales process will:

- ensure that their sales professionals identify and gather the appropriate customer information needed to define critical technical and business solutions

- ensure that their proposals clearly match their customers' needs and objectives to the proposed solutions
- differentiate their organization and its services from the competition
- reduce the time needed to write winning, customer-driven sales proposals
- ensure that all their proposals meet quality standards for content, format, and appearance
- increase their Proposal Close Ratio

In our meetings we also discussed specific sales and proposal development needs and objectives for PTI:

- establish a proposal development process that integrates with PTI's sales process
- help the sales professionals close a high volume and dollar amount of business
- design and develop standard PTI proposal models for its major practice areas
- design, develop, and integrate a client questionnaire and practice area worksheets, sales tools, to help sales professionals:

    —gather and process each customer's unique technical and business information in a consultative sales process
    —select the appropriate proposal model components to build a custom proposal for each customer situation

The purpose of this document is to propose how Daniels & Associates can assist PTI in achieving these needs and objectives.

Proposed Consulting Services

The proposed consulting services engagement will result in the design, development, and implementation of a proposal model and supporting sales tools for one (1) of PTI's software products. The following table defines proposed engagement activities.

Phase	Activities / Deliverables / Work Effort	Benefits
Requirements Definition	• Meet with PTI sales and other staff to define proposal requirements • PTI and Daniels: 1 day on-site	• gain knowledge and insight into a PTI software product • define proposal content and customer information gathering requirements
Develop Skeleton Proposal	• Develop, review, and approve a detailed skeleton proposal as a blueprint for the selected software product proposal model. • Daniels: 1 day to develop and revise • PTI: 2–4 hours to review	• the skeleton proposal is reviewed and approved by PTI staff to ensure content accuracy and development direction
Develop Proposal Model	• Write a draft software product Proposal Model and define appendices requirements based upon the approved outline. • Review the proposal model with PTI staff and make changes as needed. • Daniels: 2–4 days to develop and revise • PTI: 4–6 hours to review	• proposal development activities based upon the approved skeleton proposal • ensure that the proposal model meets quality standards and PTI's needs and objectives
Design and Develop Sales Tools	• Design and develop a PTI Customer Questionnaire and Application Worksheet for the selected software product (sales tools) based upon the approved proposal model.	• sales tools integrated with the new model proposal

Phase	Activities / Deliverables / Work Effort	Benefits
Design and Develop Sales Tools (continued)	• Review the draft questionnaire and worksheet with PTI staff and make changes as needed. • Daniels: 3–4 days to develop and revise • PTI: 4–6 hours to review	• sales tools will aid sales professionals during the sales process • sales tools reviewed and approved by PTI staff
Testing	• Test the proposal model and sales tools with a PTI sales professional and prospect. • Make final changes to the proposal model and questionnaire, if needed. • PTI and Daniels: 1 day on-site • Daniels: 1–2 days to finalize proposal model and sales tools	• ensures that the integrated sales and proposal development processes and engagement deliverables meet PTI's needs and objectives
Implementation	• Establish PTI proposal development and production procedures • Customize Daniels's *Consultative Selling and Strategic Proposals* workshop to reflect PTI's requirements • Develop a process to measure and monitor PTI's Proposal Close Ratio • Deliver the one (1) day workshop at PTI's corporate office	• ensures that PTI's sales professionals effectively use the new sales process tools and proposal model • ensures that sales results are monitored and adjustments made if needed • provides with PTI sales management with ongoing support and consulting services to meet project objectives

Phase	Activities / Deliverables / Work Effort	Benefits
Implementation (continued)	• Meet with PTI's sales management to review results on a quarterly basis for the next year • PTI: 1 day for all sales professionals and 4 days for selected sales management staff • Daniels: 2–3 days to customize the workshop materials, 1 day to deliver the workshop, and 4 days for ongoing consulting	

The first five phases of the engagement will be completed over a three-to-five-week period. Implementation will require one day. Ongoing consulting support will require four days during next year.

Fees for the entire consulting engagement are $32,000.00 plus travel expenses.

Nonfinancial Benefits

Developing a fully integrated software product proposal model and sales tools will benefit PTI's sales professionals and improve the company's overall sales process.

- Prospective customers will receive top-quality sales proposals that:

    —clearly differentiate PTI and its services, maximize the concept that PTI's software product offers exceptional technical and business solutions and
    —become the benchmark for competitive proposals.

- PTI's software product proposals will help prospective customers make buying decisions because they:

113

—position the sale as the correct software product, technical, and business strategy,

—thoroughly describe PTI's software product features and the values that they provide to each customer's unique business situation,

—contain qualitative and quantitative benefits that define how PTI's software product increases productivity and/or profitability, and discuss how PTI provides ongoing customer service and support.

- The proposed client questionnaire and practice area worksheets will help PTI's sales professionals:

    —focus and integrate their sales and proposal development activities,

    —follow an effective and consistent information gathering process, and

    —ensure the development of customer-driven sales proposals.

- The software product proposal model and sales tools developed in this engagement can be used:

    —as a basis for developing proposal models and sales tools for PTI's other software products and

    —to develop an automated proposal generation application.

- The *Consultative Selling and Strategic Proposals* workshop on-going consulting support will ensure that

    —the integrated sales and proposal development process changes are successfully implemented

    —PTI meets its project objectives

Financial Benefits

The financial benefit resulting from the development of a practice area proposal model and accompanying questionnaire lies primarily in increasing PTI's estimated and average major practice *Proposal Close Ratio* from 25% to 40% within three months.

114

PTI's Proposal Estimates and Assumptions

· Estimated Number of Software Product Proposals	100
· Average Dollar Value of a Major Practice Area	$75,000
· Estimated Current Proposal Close Ratio	25%
· Total Number of Closed Proposals	25
· Gross Revenue from Closed Proposals	$1,875,000
· Improved Proposal Close Ratio (estimated)	40%
· Total Number of Closed Proposals	40
· Gross Revenue from Closed Proposals	$3,000,000

Estimated Financial Benefits

· Annual Gross Revenue Improvement with the new PTI Integrated Sales and Proposal Development Processes	$1,125,000
· Annual Profit Improvement Based upon a 20% Pre-tax Profit Margin	$225,000
· Engagement Fee, including an estimated $4,500 of travel expenses	$36,500

Estimated 1st Year Return on Investment   **616%**

Daniels Profile

Daniels & Associates specializes in integrating complex sales processes with the development of winning strategic sales proposals. John Daniels, the firm's principal, is the author of *Strategic Selling and Proposals: How to Close the Big Deal.*

A partial list of clients includes:

· Interactive Call Response
· Talbot & Daniels
· Executive Training Centers
· Parker Regis LLP
· Prepaid Legal Services
· Newspager Comnet
· Commerce Bank of the Southwest

Engagement Schedule

The engagement can begin in early November 1999. The software product proposal model and sales tools would be ready for implementation by early December 1999. Implementation training will take one (1) day at PTI's corporate offices in early January 2000. Ongoing support will include quarterly review meetings for the next year.

Invoicing Schedule

The invoicing schedule for the initial engagement fee is as follows:

- $10,000.00 upon acceptance of this proposal
- $10,000.00 upon completion and PTI approval of a practice area model proposal and sales tools
- $12,000.00 upon completion of the proposal testing activities, plus actual travel expenses *(estimated at $4,500.00)*.

Acceptance

Please indicate your approval by signing the acceptance line below; keep one copy for your files, and return one to me.
Accepted for PTI:
By: _____
Title: _____
Date: _____

Thank you again for this opportunity to submit this proposal for your consideration. I look forward to working with you and other PTI staff in the future.

Sincerely,

John J. Daniels

11. Format and Production

The Strategic Proposal Structure

This book presents a customer-driven strategic proposal structure that the author has refined over many years of selling and consulting. It has been used to develop winning proposals for clients in different businesses and professions, ranging from executive recruiting services to machinery maintenance equipment. Each of the five interrelated main sections serves a distinct purpose as does their sequence within the proposal:

> **Section I** begins the proposal by defining a buyer improvement opportunity, the buyer's situation and the basis for the proposal.
> **Section II** presents the seller's proposed custom application of their products or services, how the seller will help the buyer achieve the improvement opportunity.
> **Section III** presents the seller's implementation methodology or project management practices and schedule to assure the buyer that the seller is able to deliver on the contract.
> **Section IV** profiles the seller's business to further assure the buyer that the seller will be able to deliver on the contract and provide ongoing service.
> **Section V** defines all the business issues: assumptions used for scheduling and pricing, how much it will cost the buyer to implement the seller's proposed solution, and when and how the seller will invoice the buyer.

Each main section incorporates supporting subsections. Like the proposal's main sections, the sequence of the subsections within each section also serves a purpose. For example, the first subsection in Section V, *Business Issues,* presents the assumptions the seller used for estimating the time and costs for implementing the proposed solution. The subsections immediately following the assumptions subsection present the schedule and fees or costs using these assumptions as their basis.

The strategic proposal contains two additional quality components, an Executive Summary and supporting appendices. The Executive Summary is a proposal in miniature. It can stand alone and gives a decision maker sufficient information to make a buying decision without having to read the entire proposal. Or more preferably, the Executive Summary focuses a recipient's attention on the proposal's message and the key points within each section. Appendices help the proposal writer control the length of the proposal and provide a place for preprinted materials.

The strategic proposal's recommended sections and subsections and components are presented on the following page as a review. The remainder of this chapter discusses techniques for enhancing the overall effectiveness of the proposal's structure and message by the use of page formatting and layout, graphics, color, etc.

Executive Summary (see chapter 9)

I. Background Information (see chapter 4)
  A. Industry Information *(optional)*
  B. Background *[buyer]*
  C. Current Operation or Functions
  D. Improvement Opportunity [definition, analysis, and plans]
  E. Needs and Objectives *[buyer]*
  F. Purpose of This Proposal
II. Proposed Solution (see chapter 5)
  A. Product or Service Description
  B. Product or Service Application *(optional)*
  B. Nonfinancial Benefits
  C. Financial Benefits
III. Implementation (see chapter 6)
  A. Engagement or Project Management Methods
  B. Schedule
  C. Team
IV. Seller Profile (see chapter 7)
  A. Mission Statement
  B. Company Profile
  C. Quality
  D. Why Us?
  E. Other subsections based on the seller's industry or profession
IV. Business Issues (see chapter 8)
  A. Assumptions

B. Fees/Prices [and other expenses]
C. Invoicing Schedule
Appendices (see chapter 9)

Select the Correct Type

Letters, numerals, symbols, and punctuation marks represent type. Selecting the correct type for the proposal is important because the wrong type can make proposal content hard to grasp while the right type can make the proposal easy to read and inviting. Type selection is important and the selling organization might seek professional advice; however, once the type layout is selected, it should be used as the standard for all proposals. Proposal teams will find following a type standard will ensure a consistent, quality appearance for the company.

There are approximately 5,000 available typefaces; however, a well-crafted proposal will use only one or two. Typefaces are grouped into families, e.g., GillSans, Arial, etc. The letterform, book, light, or regular represents the "parent." All other derivatives, e.g., bold, italics, etc., are considered "relatives." A type font represents a complete assortment of characters of one typeface in one style, such as Garamond italics.

Some guidelines to consider when selecting and using type within the proposal include:

Familiar Type. Unusual type will distract the reader from the content. Select a familiar type, such as Times Roman or Garamond for body copy.

Consistency. Choose one type family and use it for body copy and other elements with the exception of titles and section and subsection names.

Serifs. Serifs are the tiny lines that cross the ending strokes of most characters. They help the eye move easily along the line, which makes reading efficient. Use serif type, such as Times, for proposal body copy. Type without serifs, known as sans serif, works well for titles and section and subsection names.

Weight. Type is available in different weights ranging from light and book to extra bold. Use book weight for body copy and bold or extra bold for titles and section and subsection names.

Size. The height of type determines its size. Size is expressed in units called points; one point equals 1/72 inch. Use 12-point for proposal body copy, 14-point or larger for section names, and 12-point or larger for subsection names. Remember, section and subsection names use bold or extra bold weight.

Page Format and Layout

Format can drastically impact a proposal's readability. It includes page size, columns, margins. etc. Format is the proposal's form consistent with the seller's goals and objectives for visual appearance and readability. Good proposal layout ensures that sections, subsections, tables, and other elements work together for reading efficiency. One rule to follow when considering layout: *the easier it is to make, the easier it will be to read.* In other words, if the proposal writer uses a layout that is difficult to work with, then the readers also will find it difficult to read. Some guidelines to use include the following:

- Use one format throughout the proposal and one or two type faces to keep the proposal simple.
- Avoid full text pages that are difficult to read; use bullets, columns, and white space.
- Avoid elaborate headers and footers that distract from the proposal's message.

The following pages illustrate how format and layout affect readability. The first example illustrates a very plain page while the second shows how layout can invite readership.

Format and Layout: Example 1

I. Company Background: PFS

Our Understanding of PFS

Pacific Food Systems, PFS, a wholly-owned subsidiary of Pacific Enterprises, Inc., provides food distribution services to independent restaurants.

PFS has 2,500 associates, services 14,000 restaurants, has distribution points scattered throughout the western U.S., and had revenues over $2.8 billion in 1998. This was the result of delivering 3.3 million pounds of products, traveling 38 million delivery miles, and making 1.4 million deliveries.

William F. Fisher, PFS President, stated in the annual report,

The words, change, innovation, and growth describe the dynamics and challenging environment in which PFS operates. In a year characterized by constant challenges, we never faltered in our push to create productivity, while we grew our business by more than 15 percent to $2.8 billion, serviced more than 14,000 restaurant customers, while reducing 3.5 million miles from our service routes.

This shows evidence of a dynamic company, searching for ways to improve.

Substance Abuse at PFS

Measuring the magnitude and cost of alcohol or other drug (AOD) abuse is an easy calculation assuming PFS's workplace demographics follow national averages. Approximately 10 percent or 250 PFS employees are substance abusers. At an annual employer cost of $10,000 for each substance abuser, PFS's estimated annual substance abuse costs are $2,500,000.

Format and Layout: Example 2

I. Company Background: PFS

Our Understanding of PFS

Pacific Food Systems, PFS, a wholly-owned subsidiary of Pacific Enterprises, Inc., provides food distribution services to independent restaurants. PFS:

- has 2,500 associates
- services 14,000 restaurants
- had revenues over $2.8 billion in 1998; the result of
- delivering 3.3 million pounds of products

- traveling 38 million delivery miles, making 1.4 million deliveries
- has distribution points scattered throughout the western U.S.

William F. Fisher, PFS President, stated in the annual report,

The words, change, innovation, and growth describe the dynamics and challenging environment in which PFS operates. In a year characterized by constant challenges, we never faltered in our push to create productivity, while we grew our business by more than 15% to $2.8 billion, serviced more than 14,000 restaurant customers, while reducing 3.5 million miles from our service routes.

This shows evidence of a dynamic company, searching for ways to improve.

Substance Abuse at PFS

Measuring the magnitude and cost of alcohol or other drug (AOD) abuse is an easy calculation, assuming PFS's workplace demographics follow national averages.

- average percent of employees who are substance abusers: 10 percent
- annual employer cost for each substance abuser: $10,000
- PFS Associates who are substance abusers: 250
- estimated annual substance abuse cost for PFS: $2,500,000

Word-processing Software

Because of the widespread use of word-processing software, buyers now expect proposals to have a high-quality appearance. Certainly a well-crafted proposal produced on a typewriter is at a disadvantage to one with less quality but written on a personal computer and printed on a laser or ink-jet printer. Further, most top-end Mac and Windows-based word-processing software packages offer functions and features similar to those available in very sophisticated desktop publishing software. Sellers now can produce proposals with type-set quality and appearance; invariably, the competition will.

Graphics

Graphics express ideas and information through art. Graphics include: photography, typography, design graphics, and infographics.

- **Photography.** A picture can be worth a thousand words. Scanners and word-processing software makes it easy to include pictures in a proposal. Most laser or ink-jet printers can print black-and-white photographs, although, color photographs require more expensive print resources.
- **Typography.** Type represents the most basic and important elements of graphics design. Well-selected type and well-thought-out decisions regarding size, weight, line spacing, and alignment can make a proposal inviting and easy to read.
- **Design Graphics.** Design graphics includes lines, symbols, and drawings. They can enhance communication of the seller's message and make the proposal interesting and attractive. Conversely, excessive use of graphics can distract from a proposal's overall appearance and message.
- **Infographics.** Tables, charts, maps, and graphs represent infographics. The also can enhance communications and make complex concepts easier to understand. Infographics improve a proposal's readability.

Tables and Charts

Tables and charts add to a proposal's readability and help the seller achieve communications goals. Both make the proposal more interesting and enhance the seller's message.

Tables display numbers and words in rows and columns. Readers need to study tables not merely look at them to get the message. Tables condense and organize information for the proposal's readers. For example, the following table effectively communicates the seller's conversion methods; in less than one page, it defines phases and activities and deliverables for each.

CMM Phase	Phase Activities	Phase Deliverable
Conversion Analysis and Planning	• form Conversion Team • perform site survey and define custom processing requirements • finalize preliminary equipment requirements and configuration	• Equipment and Site Preparation Requirements • Telephone Line Requirements • Application Conversion Specifications
Preparation and Equipment Acquisition	• FSCS Conversion Team members *beta test* Banker 2000 • customer Conversion Team members validate and approve beta test results	• validated and approved test results
Systems Testing and Validation	• FSCS Conversion Team members *beta test* Banker 2000 • customer Conversion Team members validate and approve beta test results	• validated and approved test results
Installation and Training	• equipment installation and testing • initial customer education (on-site) using conversion test files and on-site equipment	• Phase Deliverables: *fully tested equipment, completed initial employee education*
Conversion	• final pre-conversion customer education • convert and balance; customer validation and approval • update and balance; customer validation and approval • live operation	• balanced and validated conversion • Day 1 update files • fully implemented FSCSystem Plus 2000
Quality Assurance	• on-site FSCS Conversion Liaison monitors post-conversion activities • additional customer education, as needed	• Quality Assurance Checklist

Tables can efficiently and clearly communicate exact numbers as illustrated in the example below.

D
Total Annual Return

Fund Type	1 Year	5 Years	10 Years
Growth	15.6%	14.1%	14.2%
Income	7.5%	8.1%	7.9%
Corporate Bond	5.3%	7.2%	7.4%

Pie charts show the approximate relationship of the parts to a whole. At one glance, readers can absorb the seller's message. For example, a seller might use a pie chart to show the distribution of ages in a buyer's employee population, illustrate market share within the buyer's industry, contrast major expense categories, etc. The seller should use a bar chart or line chart if they want the reader to compare data or understand precise differences.

Line charts illustrate amount changes over time. The vertical axis represents quantity and the horizontal axis represents time. For example, if your proposal needed to show a buyer's increased cost trend over the last several years, the seller might use a line chart as displayed below.

Bar charts compare amounts by using the vertical or horizontal bars to represent amounts and the sections or lines to designate quantity units. Use bar charts for comparisons of different things or to illustrate changes over time. For example, if the seller needed to compare the processing speed of their machine to competition and to the buyer's current equipment, they might use the following bar chart.

Printers

Prices for laser and inkjet printers range from less than $200 to several thousand for high-speed, high-resolution, color printers. The least expensive laser or inkjet printer can produce high-quality output. Only under the most severe budget constraints should a seller produce a strategic proposal on a dot matrix printer and then only using the near letter quality (NLQ) setting and a new ribbon.

Color

Use of color in a proposal is a function of the seller's word-processing and printing resources. Color can enhance a proposal's appearance and readability. It can do more than decorate pages, it can help achieve the seller's communications goal. A second and possibly a third text color builds contrast. For example, using colored section and subsection names helps the reader organize and categorize information. However, a word of caution: using too many text colors can slow readers down. Further, forcing the reader to switch from color to color can make the message harder to understand and remember. Conversely, use of color in tables and charts makes them easier to understand.

Paper

Upgrading paper provides one of the easiest and least costly ways to add to a proposal's quality. Since most printers and plain paper photocopiers can handle any grade, surface, or paper weight, except for high-gloss, coated, the seller can select a special paper for their proposals. Some paper considerations include:

Size. A proposal is a business document not a brochure or flyer. Use traditional size, 8½-by-11-inch paper.

Coated. Coated paper comes in different finishes: matte, dull, and gloss. It offers better ink holdout than offset or bond paper. Ink holdout refers to the extent ink dries on the surface rather than soaking into the paper. Use coated paper for proposals that contain pictures and graphics and charts with bright colors.

Offset. Offset paper is also called uncoated book paper. It's available in several shades of white and light colors and in several finishes and weights, e.g., Quality #1 is the smoothest and brightest; Quality #3 is the most frequently used. Offset paper is designed for printing on both sides, something not recommended for a sales proposal.

Bond. Paper mills produce *bond* for one-page correspondence such as letters. It works well in photocopy machines but lacks the opacity needed for two-sided printing. Since most proposals are traditionally printed on one side, bond paper will work but only in weights greater than 24#.

Weight. Paper is expressed in its weight as the weight of 500—8½-by-11-inch sheets. The higher the paper weight number, the heavier the paper and the higher its cost. Heavier weight paper also provides more opacity. Most photocopiers use 20# bond paper, which is unsuitable for a proposal. Type 24# bond is the minimum quality paper to use for a proposal.

Opacity. Opacity restricts type show through. Type from one page of a proposal should not show through to or interfere with the type on another page. Heavy papers are more opaque than lighter papers. Bond paper is not as opaque as coated paper.

Color. Paper color increases opacity but reduces legibility between the type and background. Print proposals on white or shades of white, e.g., ivory or cream. Very light tones of gray, blue, or brown also will work. Do not use dark tones for a proposal.

Surface. Paper can have a smooth or a patterned surface. Paper coatings range from dull to glossy. Spend some time at an office supply or paper store to select a quality paper with a good look and feel for the proposal. For a few extra dollars, a proposal can be printed on paper with a coating or pattern that can subtly differentiate it from the competition.

Dividers

Section dividers or tabs greatly enhance a proposal's appearance. They also add readability by helping readers categorize and find information. Use dividers for the proposal's Table of Contents, Executive Summary, and the five main sections. If the proposal uses appendices, use a divider for each. If all proposals use the same main section names, then the seller can preprint dividers. If section names change from one proposal to the next, the seller may want to use a copy center or resource that can print and insert custom dividers during the proposal's duplication process.

Some quality guidelines to follow:
Do not use:

- dividers if they will extend beyond the proposal's cover; this creates a poor quality fit and image.

- inexpensive tabs with manually typed names; it's better to use none.

Do:

- use a plastic and/or color coating on dividers to increase durability and enhance the proposal's appearance.
- print dividers using one of the fonts used within the proposal.

Binding and Covers

Except for *letter proposals,* the seller should always bind their strategic proposals. A proposal should never be bound by stapling its pages in the upper left corner. Several options, available for in-house use or through most copy centers and printers, make binding easy and inexpensive. Binding options include GBC, wire, perfect, three-ring, and others. Visit local office supply stores, copy centers, and printers to select the best proposal binding option. Two binding guidelines to follow: the selected binding should (1) make the proposal physically easy to read and (2) be durable.

A proposal's binding often determines cover selection options. For example, if the seller uses three-ring binding, the cover will be a three-ring binder. Preprinted covers enhance the overall proposal and sales message and imply buyer stability. Most binding options will allow the seller to use preprinted covers.

Number of Copies

Every decision maker and each buyer representative who is a member of the proposal team should receive an original proposal. Never send the buyer one original knowing that it will be copied, stapled in the upper left corner, and distributed to the decision makers. For a few extra dollars, the seller can send the very best to the buyer's decision makers and proposal team representatives.

Quality Production Considerations

When developing a sales proposal, form and substance play equally important roles. A strategic proposal is a business document intended to convey the seller's improvement opportunity message to the buyer in the most effective means possible. It should reflect a professional image and the seller's ability to communicate clearly and logically. The best written proposal from the most capable seller proposing the most viable solution is at risk if printed on 20# paper and stapled in the upper-left corner.

Conversely, a proposal's form should not overshadow the seller's message. For example, a partner from a leading professional services organization, when proposing a multi-million dollar engagement to one of the top mail-order catalog merchandisers in the country, decided to differentiate on form more than substance. The proposal's cover mirrored the cover from the buyer's most recent mail-order catalog. It had a model dressed in business attire holding a folder with the seller's name embossed on it. What appeared to be an impressive, client-focused proposal format backfired for the partner. The buyer knew it was costly for the seller to develop the elaborate proposal cover. The cover added no value for the buyer and the proposal did little to differentiate the seller. The buyer's decision makers felt that the seller overemphasized form while falling short on substance, a fatal combination for a professional services organization.

12. Writing the Proposal—a Partnering Process

Sales Partnerships and Proposals

Sales professionals need to form partnerships with managers and top-tier decision makers when selling to key accounts. Rarely will a partnership form after the sale; typically it forms to define the sale. The partnership creates a synergistic atmosphere because it has a mutual goal—enhancing revenues, reducing costs, and/or improving productivity of the buyer's business. It is in sharp contrast to the more common and often adversarial buyer versus seller atmosphere. Perhaps human nature also plays a role in the process.

As the partnership works towards their mutual goal, the buyer's perception of the sales professional as just another vendor changes. The sales professional becomes the buyer's consultant, because he or she uses a consultative sales approach to help define profit improvement opportunities and buyer-specific product or service application. Further, the resulting collaborative teamwork builds an attitude of trust and confidence within the partnership. The partnership's efforts produces the strategic proposal, which ultimately leads to the sale.

Integrated Processes

Consultative selling and developing strategic proposals represents integrated processes in which developing a proposal is a key part of the sales. For selling organizations that view sales proposals as the last step in the sales process, this approach requires a paradigm shift. Proposals are no longer end-products of the sales process. Rather, some sales professionals find that the more rigorous strategic proposal requirements guide their sales activities, particularly their activities involving information gathering and product or service application analysis. In many instances, the integrated processes raises the professionalism of the sales staff because it forces the selling organization and their sales professionals to enhance their consultative sales skills and strategies— critical components of successful key account sales.

Sales professionals' reactions can range from agony to excitement when asked for a proposal. Some fear that they have lost the sale if they have to write a proposal; they think a competitor must have the sale "wired." These sales professionals feel their proposal only will provide the buyer with the obligatory price comparison for signing the competitor's bid. Or they may agonize over writing proposals because they do not know how to add value for the buyer—improve the buyer's profits. Some may be selling only on price—the buyer views their products or services as commodities. Perhaps that is why so many proposals begin with a section devoted to the seller and bury the price on the very last page. These sales professionals write proposals only when buyers absolutely demand them. They view proposals as the final check-off item on their "sales to do" list; they view proposals as administrative documents.

In comparison, when sales professionals use the integrated processes approach, they are able to plan their proposals early in the sales cycle. They know that the proposal will document their consultative sales activities and the resulting buyer-seller partnership's improvement opportunity analyses. As part of the sales process, buyer and seller representatives formulate proposal content while working together to solve problems or achieve opportunities. The resulting proposal contains all the information needed by the buyer's decision makers. To these sales professionals, developing strategic proposals represents integral steps taken with the buyer during the sales process not the final step at the end of a linear process.

The Buyer-Seller Proposal Team

Because of the complexity of most complex sales, a sales professional using integrated selling and proposal development processes often must assemble and coordinate the activities of representatives for the buyer-seller partnership, the proposal team.

Buying Team Members

In his book, *Key Account Selling,* Mack Hanan identified four alliances or partnerships a sales professional may need to form within the buyer's management. These partners and their concerns are:

- **Top Management** financial, people, and operational improvement
- **Financial Management** same as Top Management's, plus investment performance
- **Functional Management** how, when, and where to improve operations
- **Purchasing** traditional price performance considerations; however, Hanan writes, "Value considerations must replace price. The financial aspects of performance must be substituted for physical, chemical, mechanical, hydraulic, or electronic performance results as buying criteria."

The *internal sponsor* or *champion,* typically a manager, acts as the sales professional's primary contact or mentor within the buying organization. Often this person also accepts the role and responsibilities of team or project manager for the buyer's team.

Selling Team Members

Even if the sales professional is an independent management consultant, he or she needs at least one additional proposal team member, a proofreader. However, in many key account sales situations, the sales professional represents a company and cannot make unilateral company commitments such as establishing subcontractor agreements, defining custom service level specifications, setting production schedules, or establishing multi-year price arrangements. Further, the size and complexity of many proposed solutions often requires that a sales professional get agreement and cooperation from others within the company. Therefore, the seller's proposal team members might include representatives who provide important proposal development and content input, representatives from production, systems development, operations, professional services, customer services, conversion services, accounting, and legal.

Depending on the proposed products or services, the seller's team members will have varying proposal development commitment levels. For example, the legal department may have no involvement unless the buyer requests a change in the contract. However, a conversion services representative would have major involvement in writing a proposal to convert the buyer to a new system. In a true buyer-seller partnership, the sales professional and his or her *internal sponsor* or *coach* co-manage proposal development project. The sales professional usually accepts the role and responsibilities of team manager for the seller's proposal writing team.

Buyer-Seller Proposal Team Roles and Responsibilities

The buyer's team members normally do not have formal roles and responsibilities in the key account selling and proposal writing. Rather, the *internal sponsor* or *coach* orchestrates the sales professional's and other seller representatives' introductions, meetings, and information-gathering activities within the buyer organization. The buyer team members usually help the sales professional develop the strategic proposal by identifying, researching, analyzing, and validating improvement opportunities. On the other hand, the seller's team members often have very formal roles and responsibilities in the proposal development process. For example, a representative from the seller's systems development department may be responsible for establishing preliminary data base specifications for a proposed systems implementation, or an accounting department representative may help the sales professional develop financial benefit calculations for the proposal.

The ability of the seller to utilize team resources represents a major benefit of the integrated processes. The sales professional can logically add selling team members to the partnership as the need for a particular expertise arises. Adding seller team members expands the buyer's exposure to the selling organization. Their teamwork geometrically expands the trust and confidence within the partnership as the team members concentrate their efforts on the buyer's improvement opportunities.

Developing a Strategic Proposal: The Steps

The following steps define timing and mechanics rather than selling, proposal development and positioning, and presentation strategies. Note that the buyer remains involved throughout the proposal development process. This involvement is most critical to the integrated sales and proposal processes's ultimate success—final buyer approval.

Step 1: Establish the Team

This step applies more to the seller's team members than the buyer's. It includes the proposal writing team's "kick-off" activities. Typical activities in this step might include defining the:

- team's purpose and the buyer's profit improvement expectations
- team member roles and responsibilities
- timeframes for the remaining steps and the actual or estimated proposal deadline
- proposal writing processes and procedures

The sales professional might hold a "kick-off" meeting to formally start the proposal development process in the seller's organization.

Step 2: Skeleton Proposal

A detailed skeleton becomes the blueprint for developing a winning proposal. The skeleton proposal should be based on this book's recommended proposal structure. If the selling organization plans to develop a proposal model and reuse it for other buyers, it should define those variables that the sales professional can change to reflect another buyer's situation. Note: Some selling organizations develop a skeleton proposal for each product or service rather than starting with a blank page for every sale.

The sales professional and the proposal writing team may want to develop a skeleton proposal and present it to the *internal sponsor* for his or her review and recommend changes. Normally, the buyer's team members do not directly participate in developing the skeleton. However, they obviously have indirect influence on content through their interaction with the seller's team members and the sales professional. Through the buyer-seller partnership, they communicate their problems, opportunities, needs, objectives, and expectations.

Some suggested skeleton proposal activities include:

- define and title main sections and subsections
- for each subsection:
    - —write a sentence describing the content or list the primary topics
    - —note buyer-specific information, such as costs, proposed solutions, benefits, etc.
    - —identify supporting appendices

Step 3: Buyer Approval

Some sales professionals call the skeleton proposal a "Strawman Proposal." It gives the seller an opportunity to solicit buyer review and approval of the proposal's logic, content, and direction with minimal development time and effort. The "Strawman Proposal" provides several benefits. It:

- gives the seller an opportunity to easily incorporate any buyer recommendations and suggestions
- begins the all important process of buyer "ownership" of the proposal, thereby enhancing the seller's chances for closing the deal
- ensures subsequent proposal development activities will be productive

Step 4: Write and Edit the First Proposal Draft

For some, the most difficult part in developing a winning strategic proposal lies in the actual writing. Certainly, the skeleton proposal helps; however, someone still has to sit down and write. Many sales professional find writing a winning strategic proposal becomes easier over time, although it is never effortless. Perhaps experience coupled with this book's recommended proposal structure will make the difference. Suggested writing and editing steps in their recommended sequence include:

- write each main section in sequence to develop a logical flow of information and ideas and ensure continuity and consistency

135

- identify supporting materials and ensure that the proposal contains accurate references
- proofread and correct the first draft
- distribute copies of the proofread first draft to the seller's proposal team and solicit their comments; if necessary, hold a team meeting to review concerns and approve the first draft

Step 5: Buyer Approval—First Proposal Draft

The sales professional should review a draft proposal with the *internal sponsor* or *champion* using a proposal marked "Draft" or "Draft Copy Only—Not For Distribution." This review step provides the seller with a "sanity check" that ensures the final proposal will meet the buyer expectations and avoid unnecessary seller surprises. The sales professional should:

- send the draft to the *internal sponsor* so he or she has sufficient time to read it and provide valid comments
- schedule a face-to-face meeting with the *internal sponsor* or *champion* to discuss his or her comments and suggestions

Step 6: Finalize and Present Proposal

After reviewing the comments and suggestions with the internal sponsor, the sales professional is able to make changes and complete the proposal. It is now ready for distribution and presentation to the buyer's decision makers.

Note: The five main proposal sections and their sequence provide an excellent basis for developing an accompanying proposal presentation. Highlighting the critical elements of each proposal section results in a presentation that parallels the proposal's flow of information and ideas. It also makes it easy for the audience to take notes in their copies of the proposal.

Step 7: Buyer Approval—the Sale

In a perfect world, buyers would sign every contract as the final step in an integrated sales and proposal development process. However, in the real world, *proposal close ratios* do not reach 100 percent; but, a sales professional who closely follows this book's recommended integrated sales and proposal development strategy could experience ratios of 40 percent or higher.

13. Implementation

Developing Strategic Proposal Process Components

The previous chapters focused on integrating a consultative sales process with a strategic proposal process and defining the characteristics of a winning, strategic proposal. However, successfully implementing a strategic proposal process requires that the selling organization first develop three integrated process components:

1. strategic sales proposal models for each product and/or service
2. a customer or client questionnaire
3. application worksheets for each product and/or service

Proposal Models

Developing a "factory approved" proposal model for each product or service results in several benefits to the selling organization:

- Key staff members from other departments can contribute to developing "factory approved" proposal models. A winning proposal will need input and approval from various departments within an organization, e.g., marketing, customer service, R&D, etc.
- Sales professionals can use the proposal models as the basis for writing custom, strategic proposals. These proposal models make it easy for sales professionals to tailor a proposal for each buying situation. Typically 20 to 30 percent of a proposal contains buyer-specific information; the remaining 70 to 80 percent is generic.
- The buyer-specific information requirements defined by the proposal models helps focus the sales professionals consultative selling activities. For example, *Section I: Background Information* contains a subsection that defines the buyer's needs and objec-

tives, which forces sales professionals to identify this information during the sales process.

Customer or Client Questionnaires

A Customer or Client Questionnaire represents a key integration tool. A questionnaire helps sales professionals gather and identify the basic buyer-specific information needed to support the organization's sales and strategic proposal development processes. To some degree, the proposal model dictates the questionnaire's design. Some buyer-specific information requirements of a questionnaire include:

- basic information: company name and address; contact names, titles, and phone numbers, etc.
- business description: industry type, number of locations, annual revenues, etc.
- business objectives and challenges that relate to the proposed product or service
- decision-making and buying processes
- key decision makers and their expectations and influences on the buying decision
- the buyer's selection criteria
- proposal presentation strategy

Application Worksheet

As its name implies, an Application Worksheet helps the sales professional define the buyer-specific application of the proposed product or service. The proposal model also dictates the design and content of this process integration tool much more than it dictates the questionnaire's. An Application Worksheet would include some of the following buyer-specific information requirements:

- application definition variables
- product features, generic benefits, and buyer-specific values
- financial benefit analyses variables, formulas, and worksheets

- implementation variables: team and schedule

Note: Selling organizations with only one or two products or services often combine the questionnaire and worksheet into one document.

Implementation Considerations

How a selling organization implements their integrated selling and proposal development processes depends upon several factors, the:

- complexity of the product or service being sold and how much its application can vary from one buyer to the next
- writing abilities of the sales force
- systems and production resources needed to meet the company's proposal appearance and packaging standards

Product or Service Complexity

Implementation of the integrated processes is challenging when a more complex product or service is being sold and/or when its application can vary significantly from one buyer to the next. In either of these situations, the selling organization should develop a model proposal(s), questionnaire, and application worksheet(s) for each product or service.

Writing Abilities of the Sales Force

The most successful sales professionals may not have the best writing abilities. Rather than trying to teach good writing skills to the entire sales force, the selling organization may want to create a proposal development function. Sales professionals would then submit completed questionnaires and worksheets to the proposal development person or group. The sales professional would be able to review and revise proposal drafts before presenting the final draft to their client. This option requires the careful design of proposal models and sales tools. It also requires the development of efficient proposal production procedures.

Systems and Production Resources Needs

If a selling organization has set proposal appearance and packaging standards that require color printing and custom covers, it may not be economically feasible to purchase the systems and equipment needed to produce proposals at branch offices. Rather, the organization may want to create a central proposal development function as discussed above. Again, the careful design of proposal models and sales tools is critically important to efficiently support branch office needs.

Sales professionals will need to complete a sales training seminar in which they:

- learn how to integrate their consultative selling skills with a strategic proposal development process
- use the proposal models and sales tools, the questionnaire and worksheets, to help develop and refine their consultative selling activities
- develop example proposals based upon representative case studies

Strategic Proposal Implementation

Designing, developing, testing, and integrating a strategic proposal and accompanying sales tools represents a significant project for most organizations. It must start with a commitment by management to change the way their sales force and the organization deals with its customers throughout the sales process. Sometime during implementation, the organization will need to buy into the integrated process approach. Some sales professionals will view the changes as a lot of unnecessary effort to elevate the importance of an administrative document. Others will embrace the integrated processes, proposals, and tools as an opportunity to raise their level of professionalism, become more consultative, and close more business.

The following project activities provide a high-level blueprint for creating a detailed plan to implement consultative sales and proposal development processes. Each selling organization is unique and should carefully evaluate their situation, needs, and objectives before undertaking the project.

Note: Do not confuse these implementation project activities with the recommended buyer-seller proposal writing process presented in the previous chapter, "Writing The Proposal—a Partnering Process."

1. **Establish the Project Team.** Select representatives from sales, marketing, and product management to participate on the project. Define roles and responsibilities.
2. **Define Project Goals and Objectives.** Ensure that all team members understand expected project outcomes. Identify affected products and services and planned project deliverables. Establish a project schedule.
3. **Develop a Strategic Proposal Skeleton.** Define and title main sections and subsections. For each subsection:

   • write a sentence describing the content or list the primary topics
   • note buyer-specific variable information, such as costs, proposed solutions, benefits, etc.
   • Identify recommended supporting appendices for each main section.

4. **Draft the Strategic Proposal Model.** Write the proposal model draft and identify those places that will require buyer-specific information. Follow the agreed upon proposal layout and format.
5. **Draft a Client Questionnaire and Application Worksheets.** Using the proposal model as the basis, reverse-engineer the Client Questionnaire and Application Worksheets.
6. **Define Process and Procedure Changes.** Define how the organization will change and integrate their sales and proposal development processes. Define strategic proposal systems requirements and production procedures.
7. **Develop Performance Measurements.** Define how the organization will measure and monitor integrated sales and proposal process performance. One recommended process effectiveness measure is the *Proposal Close Ratio*. This requires the organization to track total proposals written, won, lost, and abandoned.
8. **Test the Integrated Processes, Proposal Models, Tools, and**

Systems. Before introducing the project deliverables to the sales force, run several tests using live prospects. Review results and thoroughly debrief the sales professionals involved in the test. If possible, interview or survey the prospects, the proposal recipients, to obtain their reactions. Make project deliverable revisions as needed.

9. **Implement the Integrated Processes and Project Deliverables.** Properly positioning the integrated processes, proposals, procedures, tools, and systems with the sales professionals is critical. Simply presenting these changes and materials to the sales force and expecting immediate acceptance and use is a formula for disaster. Rather, develop and deliver a workshop in which the sales professionals get hands-on experience with the proposal models and accompanying tools using case study examples. Part of the implementation phase should also include an introductory period during which the sales professionals can receive additional support.

10. **Monitor Results.** Monitoring integrated sales and strategic proposal development process results is an ongoing activity for the entire organization. Use the performance measurements established during this project to constantly evaluate process effectiveness and publish the results.

Automation—*The Next Phase or the Next Project?*

The strategic proposal structure and supporting sales tools presented in this book provide a solid foundation for process automation. As stated earlier, client-specific information typically represents 20 to 30 percent of a strategic proposal's content. This is the information sales professionals capture and develop using their consultative selling skills and the supporting sales tools. The remaining 70 to 80 percent of a proposal's content is comprised of standard wording contained in the proposal model. By transferring and combining the client-specific information on the sales tools with the standard wording on the proposal model, the seller can create a custom, strategic proposal. The process is totally manual if the tools and proposal model are paper-based. However, it is possible to automate the processes if the:

- sales tools were developed into application input screens and
- proposal model was converted into a database file or a word-processing document containing input fields for variable information.

An automated proposal system allows a sales professional to input and process client-specific information on his or her computer throughout the sales process. To get a draft proposal, he or she simply presses a button and the system automatically prints a custom proposal. Assuming he or she had conscientiously followed a consultative sales approach, the resulting draft proposal would be 95+ percent complete; ready for review and final changes.

Developing an automated proposal system will clearly show the selling organization that its consultative selling and strategic proposal development processes must be fully integrated to be synergistic. Design deficiencies in the sales tools and proposal model will limit a sales professional's ability to gather and process appropriate client information. Or if a sales professional is not truly consultative, then the client information input to even the best-designed sales tools will lack substance. In either or both situations, the resulting proposals will lack the compelling reasons for the buyer to make a change.

Epilogue

Developing a strategic proposal model and supporting sales tools may be less arduous than you might think. Most of what you need to put in your proposal will deal with things you already know about—your products or services, your company, and how you do business. Remember to enlist support from others within your company, e.g., marketing, production, etc. The most difficult task might be deciding what you need to know about a client to clearly define the product or service application and the resulting financial and nonfinancial benefits. Closely follow this book's recommended structure and content specifications; they have worked well for all sizes and types of organizations. Use the examples for ideas on how to design your proposal model and sales tools.

When you begin to integrate your consultative selling and proposal development processes two things should happen: you will (1) raise your level of selling professionalism and (2) increase your *Proposal Close Ratio*. If you use the new sales tools to help guide you through parts of your sales process activities, your clients will perceive you as a consultant or business partner, not another vendor. They will start listening to what you have to say because you will be helping them achieve an improvement opportunity; you will not be simply reciting the features of your product or capabilities of your service. More important, because your new proposals will capture the results of your consultative selling activities, your clients will be better prepared to move forward. Specifically, your client's top management, the ultimate decision makers, will have all the information they need to evaluate your proposed business solution. You may find that when your clients can make informed buying decisions, the decisions will be more forthcoming, whether they are positive or negative.

You should also experience an increase in your *Proposal Close Ratio.* How much of an increase should you expect? If you are closing 25 percent of your proposals now you may easily move the ratio up to 35 or 40 percent. Some companies may experience phenomenal increases in the number of closed deals; their close ratios may rise to 50 or even 75 percent. The increase will be because you have become more consultative and your proposals present client-specific business solutions that will help clients achieve their improvement opportunities. Perhaps the increased proposal close ratio represents the true measure of the synergy resulting from the integration of your consultative selling and proposal development processes.

Bibliography

Alessandra, Tony, and Rick Barrera. *Collaborative Selling.* New York: John Wiley & Sons, 1993.

Bosworth, Michael. *Solution Selling.* Chicago, Illinois: Irwin Professional Publishing, 1995.

Finkler, Steven A. *The Complete Guide to Finance & Accounting for Non–Financial Managers.* Englewood Cliffs, New Jersey: Prentice-Hall, 1983.

Hanan, Mack. *Consultative Selling.* New York: AMACOM, 1990.

———. *Key Account Selling.* New York: AMACOM, 1993.

Hilton, Ronald W. *Managerial Accounting.* New York: McGraw-Hill, 1991.

Kantin, Robert, and Mark Hardwick. *Quality Selling through Quality Proposals.* Cincinnati, Ohio: International Thomson Publishing, 1994.

Miller, Robert, and Stephen Heiman. *Strategic Selling.* New York: Warner Books, 1985.

Rackham, Neil. *Major Account Sales Strategy.* New York: McGraw-Hill, 1989.

Thomsett, Michael C. *Winning Numbers.* New York: AMACOM, 1990.

Willingham, Ron. *Integrity Selling.* New York: Doubleday, 1987.

About the Author

Robert F. Kantin is president of KEI and Associates, a consulting firm specializing in sales and proposal process integration and automation. For more information about their consulting services, visit their Web Site: www.salesproposals.com.

"This book is an essential tool for all professionals and organisations who are required to submit written proposals to win sales and contracts. Application of the principles presented in the book will result in a significant increase in proposal/close ratios.

"In today's business world, whether within a service, manufacturing, or government environment, "successful selling" is critical to survival. This book is a 'step-by-step' guide to developing customised winning sales proposals, which integrates a consultative sales process with the development of a strategic proposal. It identifies the characteristics of a winning strategic proposal and guides readers in developing consultative relationships with potential buyers. Obtaining critical qualitative and quantitative information is required to demonstrate an understanding of how the 'product' will add value to current strategies, the financial impact of the seller's product, and the critical decision-making tools used by top management.

"The approach recognises and reflects the realities of today's team-based selling and buying process that buyers need to make informed comparisons between competitors and options.

"This book provides numerous relevant examples to help readers integrate and apply the principles presented to their specific work environments. The emphasis placed on early and ongoing involvement of the buyer in the proposal development process will ensure the proposal clearly identifies and demonstrates not only the value added benefits of the product, but also the capacity of the seller to uniquely deliver on the contract."

—Cathie Kennedy
Principal Consultant
The Australian Institute of Management
B.A., Grad.Dip.App.Psy., M.A.Ps.S., M.B.A.

"*Strategic Proposals* is an immediately understandable and applicable book both for seasoned veterans and novice account managers. A clear overall structure for proposals is offered with detailed recommendations. For the skeptics a clearly stated logic for each recommendation is offered. Perhaps its greatest strength, however, is its use of stories and real cases to communicate how to develop successful proposals. You will find this a useful book and your customers will certainly agree."

—Dr. William L. Cron
Professor of Marketing
Edwin L. Cox School of Business
Southern Methodist University

"After reading your book, I realized that our proposals did not reflect our consultative sales process. We redesigned our property and rental management proposals using this book's recommended structure and guidelines. We now do a much better job of educating prospective property owners and investors about all aspects of the strategic, long-term decisions they are making. This book will help any organization focus their consultative selling activities."

—Robert E. Milne
President, The Resort Company

"Many sales people use boilerplate proposals to package the price along with generic features and benefits and seller information. In strong contrast, this book presents a practical approach that links consultative selling to the development of a very customer-specific sales proposal. It presents a logical proposal structure and describes in detail how each component will help the customer make a buying decision.

Perhaps the use of a model proposal and supporting sales tools to write strategic proposals is the most innovative concept presented in the book. Any size organization will find this approach an effective way to implement a strategic proposal process that helps focus the consultative selling efforts of their sales force."

—Gary B. Elliott, M.D.
President, IntelliMail

152

"Besides selecting the right software, a successful proposal automation project has three critical components: 1) designing an effective proposal model; 2) developing a customer information gathering tool; and 3) integrating the proposal development process with a consultative sales process. *Strategic Proposals* provides a clear and concise guide for accomplishing all three. This book should be essential reading for any organization that wants to automate its proposal process and increase its proposal close ratio."

—Michael Damphousse
Vice President of Marketing
Co-founder, Pangaea

"This is one of the most perceptive books I have read on selling; it provides real-world structures, examples, and guidelines. Any sales professional who follows a consultative sales process needs this book as a reference. It clearly links selling and writing a winning sales proposal; combined processes I think many organizations would find most beneficial."

—Ruben S. Cortez
President, Recruiting Resources, Inc.
Executive and Management Consultants